# WORD PROCESSING

Vera Hughes is a partner in DEVA WP, specialising in word processing consultancy, training and bureau services. She is a member of the British Computer Society (Office Automation sub-group), and worked for three years as a Senior Training Adviser for the Manpower Services Commission, for whom she prepared a guidance booklet on *Word Processing Training in Schools and Colleges*. Her experience ranges from setting up and conducting WP courses for young people and those returning to office work, to advising on and providing in-house staff training on a variety of WP systems.

TEACH YOURSELF BOOKS

# WORD PROCESSING

Vera Hughes

TEACH YOURSELF BOOKS

Hodder and Stoughton

*First published 1985*
*Third Impression 1987*
*Fourth Impression 1988*
*Fifth Impression 1988*

*British Library Cataloguing in Publication Data*

Hughes, Vera
Word processing. – (Teach yourself series)
1. Word processing
I. Title
652′.5     HF5548.115

ISBN 0 340 37627 9

*Printed and bound in Great Britain for*
*Hodder and Stoughton Educational,*
*a division of Hodder and Stoughton Ltd,*
*Mill Road, Dunton Green, Sevenoaks, Kent,*
*by Richard Clay Ltd, Bungay, Suffolk.*
*Photoset by Rowland Phototypesetting Ltd,*
*Bury St Edmunds, Suffolk.*

# Contents

**Guide to the Assignments** vii

**Preface** ix

**1 What is Word Processing?** 1
Processing words – from manuscript to WP. The word processor – machine or person? Word and data processing. Graphics. Does word processing 'de-skill' the operator? Word processing and other developments.

**2 What Can Word Processing Do?** 16
Processing text. Processing figures and forms. Basic and advanced WP functions and features.

**3 How Does Word Processing Work?** 47
Hardware. Software. Configurations. Compatibility. Storage media. Accessories. Stationery.

**4 The Word Processing Environment** 83
Furniture. Lighting. Atmosphere. Décor. People. Tidy working.

**5 How to Start Word Processing** 90
Getting started. Screen messages. Command and edit. Opening a file (creating a document). Document-based and page-based systems. Menu- and code- or command-based systems. The three stages of WP. Assignments 1 and 2. Closing down.

**6  Gaining Experience**                                    121
    Assignments 3–11 (*see* Guide to the Assignments)

**7  Managing the WP System**                                157
    Office procedures. Housekeeping procedures.

**8  Word Processing Pitfalls**                              181
    Losing work. Keying in, editing and amending work.
    Printing out.

**9  WP Knowledge, Skills and Aptitudes**                    192

**Glossary of WP Terms**                                     198

**Index**                                                    207

# Guide to the Assignments

**Assignment 1**                                                         109
    Correcting common errors.
**Assignment 2**                                                         111
    Keying in text. Paragraphing. Making simple
    amendments. Printing out.
**Assignment 3**                                                         121
    Setting margins. Emboldening. Underlining.
    Right-hand justification. Printing out. Adjusting
    margins.
**Assignment 4**                                                         125
    Setting tabs. Keying in tabulated work. Altering
    tabs. Storing work on disk (if not done automati-
    cally).
**Assignment 5**                                                         129
    Recalling a document from disk. Making an amend-
    ment. Saving the *amended* version.
**Assignment 6**                                                         131
    Using indented paragraphs. Printing out on headed
    paper. Printing an envelope or label.
**Assignment 7**                                                         135
    Centring. Using flush right facility. Using tempor-
    ary storage facility (buffer memory).
**Assignment 8**                                                         138
    Moving blocks of text. Global search and replace.
    Automatic page numbering.

**Assignment 9**                                               146
   Form letter/mail merge.
**Assignment 10**                                              149
   Wide screen (landscape). Centre tabs and decimal
   tabs. Vertical lines.
**Assignment 11**                                              153
   Double-column work.

# Preface

Word processing is now used extensively in offices of all types, and by many people in their homes. It is also taught in schools and colleges, yet there are still many thousands of people who know it only as something which goes on in the office somewhere, and something they would like to know more about.

This book is designed for those who know little or nothing about word processing, but who would like to know more: employed secretaries and typists; people returning to office work after a period of absence; people who run small businesses and are considering introducing word processing; people who are learning secretarial skills.

The best way of teaching yourself word processing is to have access to a word processor and to practise using it – much of this book is written to be used in conjunction with a machine and its training and instruction manuals. For those without access to a machine, the book should nevertheless provide a sound background knowledge of the principles of word processing and how it works.

## Acknowledgments

My most grateful thanks to my partner, David Weller, for his support and encouragement and for 'processing' all the words I have written, and to Kevin Stickings for the illustrations – the 'graphics', one might say.

The assignments in this book, with additional teaching notes, have been produced as masters in A4 format for class use by teachers and lecturers. Entitled *Learning Word Processing*, by Vera Hughes, they are available only direct from DEVA WP, The Studio, Rear of 130 Burnt Ash Road, Lee, London SE12 8PU (tel: 01-318 2072), to whom all enquiries should be addressed.

# 1

# What is Word Processing?

## Processing words – from manuscript to WP

Word processing is exactly what those two words, 'word processing', themselves imply – the processing of words, or text. Indeed
word processing is often referred to as text processing and these two
expressions are interchangeable, although word processing is the
more commonly used. It is also often referred to simply as WP. So
word processing, WP, or text processing all mean the same thing.
But what *do* they mean?

People have been using the written word to convey information
for centuries and the success or failure of the communication has
depended upon two main elements: first, the actual *content* of the
communication, and second, the *means* by which that content is
conveyed from the transmitter of the information to the receiver.
Word processing is about the latter – the means by which information, expressed in words, is conveyed. The content of any piece
of information is still dependent upon the skill of the originator or
author of the words in putting those words together in phrases,
sentences, paragraphs and documents. Word processing is the
means used to convey the message.

Manuscript (handwriting) and printing were until towards the
end of the last century the main methods of written communication.
At that time use of the typewriter became more widespread; it has
remained in essence unchanged until comparatively recently.

The clatter of the 'manual' typewriter was a familiar sound in
every office, and where vast quantities of typewritten material were
required, typing pools were set up to 'process' the flow of words

more efficiently. The manual typewriter is still a feature of many an office – not just for when the power fails, but as an integral part of the communication process. Manual typewriters are gradually disappearing, of course, and the market in new manual typewriters is now confined almost exclusively to portable machines. In the 1950s and 1960s the electric typewriter gradually became the 'in' thing to have around the office.

The advantages of an electric typewriter were considered by many to be over-rated, particularly by those who could never come to terms with the keys 'running away with them', the lightness of touch required and all those mistakes which appeared as if by magic on the typescript. However, the reduction in finger fatigue, the quietness, the evenness of the typescript, the repeat keys and other features which were gradually introduced, and above all the appearance of the finished typed page – the quality of the output – very soon established the electric typewriter as preferable to the manual typewriter.

They were, and are, both machines of course – machines used to convey the written word clearly and efficiently.

The pursuit of easy use and better quality output continued. What more irritating than having to re-type a whole page for one mistake? So the self-correcting ribbon was introduced. The methods of emphasis – underlining (or underscoring, as the teachers of typewriting will have it), spacing and centring, always in the same typeface – seemed after all those years to be unimaginative and boring, and so the golf ball came along. At last one could change the typeface with ease and make the typescript look that much more attractive. The fading fabric ribbon, too, gave place to the carbon ribbon – expensive, but so much better to look at; and rubbers gave way to correcting fluid – so that the carbons were never properly corrected. Progress in the means of written communication? Yes – and improvement in ease of use and quality of output. The skill of the typist was still very much required – in accuracy, layout, spelling, grammar, speed and all the other skills which were needed to produce immaculate typewritten material.

Then at the end of the sixties and in the early seventies came the breakthrough. The microchip and the typewriter came together, the typewriter was 'computerised' and the word processor with its keyboard, screen and disk drive was born.

**Fig. 1.1** A typical word processor

So a word processor is a glorified typewriter? Well, yes, but it is so much more than that, and getting more sophisticated and powerful every year – or every time a new product is launched upon the office world. The first thing that distinguishes a word processor from a typewriter above all else is its memory – the ability of the machine, given certain commands, to store in its memory text which has been 'typed' or 'keyed' in. The second great distinguishing feature is the machine's ability, again given the right commands, to manipulate text so that correction, amendment or revision are easy. Notice that in each case – memory and manipulation of text – the right commands have to be given. It is only a machine, and will do exactly what it is told, no more and no less: the old computer maxim GI = GO (garbage in = garbage out) holds good for word processors just as much as it does for any other form of computer. So it follows that the skills and knowledge needed in typewriting are still required in word processing, and further skills and knowledge will need to be acquired. The word processor is a machine which enables the operator to produce written communication with an ease and to a quality which was not possible on the typewriter, whether manual or electric.

Between the typewriter and the word processor has emerged the electronic typewriter. It has, to a limited extent, some of the features of a word processor – it usually has a small amount of memory, and often the facility for easy correction of errors. The quality of its output is as high as that of many word processors, and, indeed, better than some whose printout facilities are inadequate. The electronic typewriter certainly has its niche in the office equipment scene, depending on the use to which it is to be put, but it is not as powerful nor as versatile as a true word processor, and is not intended to be.

## The word processor – machine or person?

There is, inevitably, a specialised vocabulary emerging with word processing, and various common word-processing terms will be used and explained throughout this book. The glossary of terms at the end summarises those that are most in use. The list is not exhaustive, as new terms are still being invented, and, as with all language, only time will standardise and stabilise the WP jargon. Suffice it to say at this juncture that the term 'word processing' normally means the input, manipulation and output of words or text; a word processor is the machine on which these functions are performed; a word processor operator is the person who works the machine. However, even now these terms are merging and changing. A person will often be referred to as 'a word processor' or a 'WP operator', and in many offices the person who spends most of his or her time (mostly 'her') operating a word processor is called, simply, 'the WP', just as if she were the machine itself! This may not be an altogether unreasonable way of looking at it because the best machine in the world is no use without a competent operator – 'the WP' – as long as it is clearly remembered that 'the WP' *is* a person and *not* just a machine.

So 'the word processor' has widened its meaning in the very short space of time it has been used in offices to include the person who works the machine as well as the machine itself, no matter what the size or capacity of the machine, nor the job title of the person. Word processing is also broadening its base and becoming part of many information processing functions. An important aspect of this extension is the relationship between word and data processing.

## Word and data processing

Computers have been part of business and manufacturing life, and of the administrative processes which serve industry, for many years now. The history of the computer, its clumsy beginnings and rapid growth in versatility and capacity, at the same time as its reduction in size, is well documented.

The job titles of the people working with computers – systems analysts, programmers, data processors – are also familiar terms, although what each person actually does is not universally understood. This is partly the result of a certain mystique which surrounded computer users in the early days and on into the fifties and sixties. They seemed to work odd hours, they dressed differently from office workers and their workplace was always cool in summer and warm in winter (for the sake of the machines, of course, not the people!). Data processing was – and is – the processing of data, just as word processing is the processing of words. In the processing of data certain jargon terms emerged, working patterns became established (although constantly changed as improvements were made), and a whole computer industry was born and now flourishes.

But a word processor (the machine) is a computer, too, isn't it? Yes it is, and the worlds of WP and DP are merging. Although a WP operator may spend most of the time processing text, on occasions there is data to be handled. This does not mean just keying in figures as part of a WP document, but using computer programs which would normally be regarded as data rather than text. For this, somewhat different disciplines are needed in the use of the

The normal monthly trading results, broken down by branch and department, show a marked increase in sales in Department A, with an overall increase of 7.5%. Each branch has made its contribution to this increase.

MAY TRADING RESULTS

| BRANCH | DEPT A | DEPT B | DEPT C | DEPT D |
|--------|--------|--------|--------|--------|
| CATFORD | 89.12 | 907.34 | 512.98 | 673.65 |
| LEWISHAM | 343.49 | 674.87 | 298.35 | 473.51 |
| ELTHAM | 896.67 | 291.75 | 483.74 | 538.27 |
| FOREST HILL | 67.38 | 78.84 | 45.18 | 92.46 |
| SHORTLANDS | 174.68 | 381.63 | 253.97 | 383.69 |
| % +/- | +7.5% | +1.7% | -2.4% | +2.3% |

The decrease in sales in Department C (- 2.4%) is mainly the result of very poor figures from Forest Hill. The reasons for this are well-known and need not be enumerated here. It is believed that JUNE's figures will show some improvement.

**Fig. 1.2** The merging of words and data

keyboard – the keyboard itself is the same, but it may be that the same key will perform a different function for DP from the function it performs for WP. There is no real reason why a WP operator should not, as the occasion arises, become a DP operator for a short while, so that the data and the text can be merged into one document, if that is what is required. For example, a company report will often require information in words (the textual explanation of the matter in hand) supported by figures (the appropriate data held in the company's computer).

It is much more efficient for the same operator to be able to handle both the word and the data processing sides of the report, and so, for a while, the two disciplines come together on the same machine, in the same document, processed by the same person. Conversely, there are occasions when a DP operator will need to become, for a while, a WP operator. But surely the DP operator will not have all the skills of a competent WP operator? Well, no; just as the WP operator will not have all the skills of a competent DP operator. However, the DP operator who is, after all, a skilled keyboard operator, is quite capable of keying in a certain amount of text and making sure that the whole document – incorporating data and text – is correctly printed out. An operator working in an insurance company, for example, who is used to handling the figures involved in insurance quotations, can easily key in a client's name and address and other variables (words) and print out and despatch the quotation to the client. Again the DP and WP functions have merged. These operators are sometimes known as WP clerks – yet another job title!

## Graphics

There is a third dimension to the processing of information – graphics. Graphics is the term used to cover every form of 'drawing' on the screen, from the vertical and horizontal lines required to create a simple form, to the highly complicated and sophisticated illustrations needed for scientific and technical documents.

As the machines, and the computer programs which run them, become yet more versatile, so graphics is (or are?) becoming within the reach and capabilities of the WP operator. Charts and graphs, as well as text and data, can be incorporated in the same document on

*T.R.Smith & Company.*

112 HILTON WAY,
EDGBURY, LANCS.
TELEPHONE: 061-239-6877.

| TO: | | INVOICE NO: | |
| --- | --- | --- | --- |
| | | DATE: | |
| | | VAT NO: | |

TERMS 30 DAYS NET

| QUANTITY | DESCRIPTION | UNIT PRICE | TOTAL |
| --- | --- | --- | --- |
| | | | |
| | | | |
| | | | |
| | | | |
| | | | |

**Fig. 1.3**   Simple graphics with lettering

the same machine, by the same person. It is also becoming possible
for the machine itself, given the right instructions, to convert data
into chart or graph form, without the operator having to draw or
create the required illustration. It is not the intention here to
describe in detail how data and graphics can be processed by the
operator. The book, after all, is about word processing. It is
important, however, to realise how word processing is becoming a
part of information processing, and that the mastery of word
processing is an excellent introduction to the broader and very
exciting field of information processing.

## Does WP 'de-skill' the operator?

One of the aims of introducing computers to information processing
which has often been stated, particularly by manufacturers and

distributors, is to increase productivity; this it can certainly do. Something it can also do, and often succeeds in doing, is to reduce the drudgery of office work. This should become apparent when the applications and techniques of word processing are studied in detail later in the book. While word processing can help to eliminate or minimise some of the drudgery of office work, it has been seen – and feared – in some quarters as 'de-skilling' the operator. How can a 'machine minder' – which is how some people regard a WP operator – display to the best advantage the talents and skills of creativity and an ability to be accurate? It was easy enough on a typewriter to distinguish a 'good' typist from a 'poor' one – if a letter was accurate and looked good and was completed in reasonable time, then the worth of the typist was self-evident. Likewise, shoddy work and a waste-paper basket full of re-types could be ascribed directly to the skills (or lack of them) of the typist. Yet the abilities of the WP operator do show through in the finished work, although the methods of attaining perfect copy are different.

It is true that, like the electric and electronic typewriter, the electronic keyboard and the printer eliminate the possibility of variability in touch – the page of typescript always comes out looking even, whatever you do, unless you use a very faded fabric ribbon. However, what you *can* do – and this is where the expert operator is distinguished from the inexpert – is use layout and display skills which were impossible on the typewriter, so that each piece of work is displayed in the style appropriate to its status with headings and display used to enhance the appearance and give emphasis where required.

It is also true that mistakes can be easily corrected on the WP, so that first-time accuracy is no longer necessary. However, it will very soon become apparent that an inaccurate operator will spend an inordinate amount of time correcting mistakes, assuming that they are actually found – proof-reading is every bit as important as it was.

So, both display skills and accuracy are still required. But what about creativity? Word processing is building up a very curious (but welcome) relationship with other forms of lettering and then with the photocopier. Word processing machines can imitate typefaces normally associated with printing; letterheads, logos and other distinguishing features can be created using various lettering. Combine these with printout from the word processor, some judicious

# DEVA WP

**WORD PROCESSING — SERVICES & TRAINING**

D I R E C T O R Y

O F

S E R V I C E S

W O R D   P R O C E S S I N G   B U R E A U

P H O T O C O P Y I N G

T H E R M A L   B I N D I N G

S P E C I A L I S E D   T R A I N I N G

**Fig. 1.4**   Lettering and word processing are combined via the
photocopier

cutting and pasting and imaginative use of the photocopier, and very satisfactory results can be achieved for front pages, contents pages, pages requiring illustrations, etc.

Word processing, then, does not 'de-skill' the operator. It can help improve the performance of the poor operator and can release the good operator to use flair and imagination in the production of perfect copy. It is rather like acting – first get the words and the techniques right, and then you use your talents and skills to bring the whole thing to life.

## Word processing and other developments

What, then, is the future of word processing? It is unwise, if not impossible, to predict the precise developments which will take place in the next ten years. If one thing seems certain, it is that word processing as such will spread more and more rapidly throughout the office world. At the same time it will extend its fields of operation into many different means of processing information, where word processing techniques, if not pure word processing, will be needed.

As improvements are made and different computers become increasingly able to 'talk' to each other, then the amount of information (text, data and graphics) which can be sent from one person to another, one company to another, one country to another and one continent to another will itself increase.

It is still written, as opposed to verbal, communication with which we are dealing. Verbal and visual communication across the world has been with us in many forms for many decades, but the ability to send written information electronically across the world is still developing.

### Fax
Facsimile transmissions of documents (fax) are growing in popularity. The document is fed into the transmitting machine where it is 'read' by the machine and converted into 'language' which is understood by telephone apparatus. It is then sent via the telephone lines to the receiving fax machine and 'translated' back into the image that a human being can understand.

Copies of documents, illustrations, diagrams, sketches, photographs, etc., can be transmitted in this manner. Special compatible

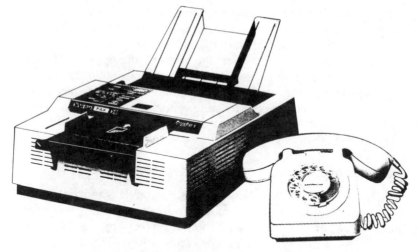

**Fig. 1.5**    A fax machine – linked by telephone

machines are required at both ends of the communication channel, linked by a telephone line.

Fax has nothing directly to do with word processing, except that documents created on word processors are often transmitted by the fax system. Word processors or information processing machines can, however, transmit text, data and graphics direct from one machine to another without first having the document printed out on paper.

**Electronic messages and mail**
This can happen within a building, between companies or world-wide. Within a company in the same building this means that the necessity for paper memoranda diminishes, and that the secretary no longer has to run down three flights of stairs to leave a message on someone's desk. Messages can be left for staff who are temporarily away, either via their own desk-top computer, or at a terminal common to many users. The essence of this service is that it should be easily accessible and that the recipient of the message can read it quickly.

The message sender and the message receiver both need a computer terminal with which to 'talk' to each other. In one company on one site this is more than likely to be so; in one company on several sites it is also probable (although by no means certain) that equipment on the different sites will be compatible. What is less likely is that computer terminals used by different companies will be able to 'talk' to each other. Machines made by different manufacturers are normally not able to communicate with each other without the use of a converter or 'modem', and so electronic mail, which is possible, is by no means as widespread as it could be. The ability to send letters and other documents electronically, without using the postal services, is alluring; it is a facility which the WP operator will increasingly be able to use.

### Telex

Another efficient transmitter of information is the telex system – many typists use it as an everyday communication tool. As telex, too, becomes electronic and computerised, it will mean that screen will speak to screen, messages can be stored and sent overnight, the 'clatter' of the telex machines will cease. Indeed, throughout the office world the clatter of machinery is giving way to the 'bleep' of the computer. It will be interesting to see whether this has any lasting psychological effects.

### The electronic diary

One of the most time-consuming and difficult tasks that an office worker has to perform is to arrange meetings. Even if 'teleconferencing' – meetings by people at different locations but able to see and talk to each other – is the means by which the meeting is to take place, the people still have to be assembled at the same time on the same day. Many hours are spent on the telephone with diaries at the ready. The introduction of the electronic diary system can, therefore, greatly reduce the drudgery of that particular task. The diary of each person due to attend the meeting can be called up and checked for availability and the meeting arranged and recorded in the diary.

This is, of course, quicker and easier, but still does not take account of the person who forgets to enter an engagement in the diary in the first place – the computer is only a machine, not a mind-reader. Where does word processing fit into this particular piece of office automation? Again, familiarisation with office computers and WP techniques will be required to call information to the screen, manipulate it and store it for future use.

### Information storage and retrieval
Indeed, the storage and retrieval of information of all descriptions is an important part of every business, from price catalogues to sales records to clients' names and addresses and many other 'databases'. The WP operator is in an ideal position to handle this information storage and retrieval, which in many ways forms an integral part of the word processing function.

### Voice input
Many keyboards have been mentioned in this chapter, from manual typewriter to telex machinery, but will the keyboard itself become redundant? When will it be possible to speak into a machine and for the words (verbal communication) to be transformed into 'printing' on paper (written communication)? It has been possible to do this for some time, but in a very elementary and, so far, unsatisfactory way. The machine has to identify sounds and convert them into typescript; it has to separate one word from another, one sentence from another. Consider the slovenly way in which many people speak – whatever the language; vowel sounds are impure, words and even sentences are run together. So it seems likely that it will be many years before voice input will be able to be widely used and that the keyboard will be with us for some time yet. Development is slow, and the leap from 'prototype' to 'mass production' is difficult.

This is true of many of the information processing techniques mentioned in this chapter. For example, the technology exists to combine text, data and graphics on one machine by one person into one document, but the spread of the technology is slower than many have predicted. Above all, businesses must be able to see that a new product is going to be cost-effective and at a price they can afford. Until big business, and then medium-sized businesses and finally small businesses can buy and use the new products, then not all the exciting developments will be available to all the office workers who would like to use them.

The brief look in this chapter at what the future may hold for word processing is not intended to deter the new operator – word processing is an excellent way into the world of information processing and office automation.

The transmission and reception of information all over the world is becoming faster and more efficient. Whether the information and the use that is made of it is becoming more effective is quite another question and one which emphasises the distinction to be made between the quality of the information, be it text, data or graphics, and the means by which it is transmitted. Anyone who knows how to use these methods of transmitting information – and the WP operator can be among the foremost of these – will find their skills and knowledge more and more in demand as the technology continues to improve and expand.

# 2

# What Can Word Processing Do?

As mentioned in the previous chapter, word processing can not only take the drudgery out of much repetitive, office written communication work, it can also be used in a creative, imaginative way. The appearance of work produced on a word processor equals, and often exceeds, that produced on the best electric and electronic typewriters. Remember, therefore, that in all the applications of word processing mentioned in this chapter, the finished product will, if the machine is properly used, be of excellent quality – in appearance at least.

It is also important to remember that whilst every word processor has certain basic facilities, such as ease of correction and text editing, the variety of functions will differ from machine to machine. For example, it is possible to 'draw' vertical lines on one machine, but not on the next. The facilities available on each machine depend first upon the memory capacity of the machine and second, upon the way in which the word processing 'software' is written. Software is the program of instructions which enables the machine to work – this is explained in more detail in Chapter 3.

## Processing text

Let us first look at the type of work for which word processing is particularly suitable, with a short explanation of how each is achieved. This falls into four main categories:

1  **Bulk mailing**  Work requiring many copies of almost identical text.

2 **Document compilation**   Work requiring the same text to be used fairly frequently, but with substantial variable information inserted.

3 **Drafting**   Single documents which require several drafts.

4 **Updating**   Documents which are long-lasting but require frequent or occasional amendment.

For each of these categories the work must first be keyed in, which is the most time-consuming part of the operation. The work can then be stored in the computer's memory and re-called as often as necessary. Amendments can be made and the documents printed out as required. These steps can be summarised as:

Input
Storage
Retrieval
Amendment
Printout

The way in which they are processed depends upon the application for which the WP is used.

### 1   Bulk mailing

It is often necessary to send out several copies of the same letter or other document with names and addresses, dates, times, etc., the only variable information required.

There are two ways of achieving this, and the method used will depend upon the number of letters to be sent out and the facilities available on the machine.

The first method is often called *form letters* and the second *mail merge*, although the latter is sometimes called *list processing*.

**Form letters**   It may be that you need to send out several letters, ten for example, to different people giving slightly different information in each. Perhaps you wish to ask candidates to attend for a job interview, or write to let job applicants know that they have not been selected for the job.

In each case you would want your letter to be a 'personal' letter written to that person alone. The text of the letter would be the same, but the name, address and salutation (Dear Mr, Mrs, Miss, Ms, etc.) would be different. In the case of asking applicants to

```
The Accounts Manager
*


*


Dear Sir

                    ACCOUNT NO:  *

According to our records, the amount(s) indicated below are still
outstanding.  We should be grateful if you would give this matter
your urgent attention and settle our account without delay.


         Invoice No        Invoice Date        Amount Payable
             *                 *                    *




Yours faithfully



Martin Gregory
CREDIT SALES MANAGER
```

**Fig. 2.1**   Form letter with spaces for variables marked

# A. R. LUKES & Co. Ltd.

BOUNDARY WORKS
SILLOTH WAY
CARLISLE
CUMBRIA

The Accounts Manager
Salco PLC
28-30 Factory Road
BOLTON
Greater Manchester
BL2 7FG

30 April 1986

Dear Sir

ACCOUNT NO:  S 2072 418

According to our records, the amount(s) indicated below are still
outstanding.  We should be grateful if you would give this matter
your urgent attention and settle our account without delay.

| Invoice No | Invoice Date | Amount Payable |
|------------|--------------|----------------|
| 2072 567   | 29/1/86      | £2,629.19      |
| 2072 668   | 28/1/86      | £1,248.20      |

Yours faithfully

Martin Gregory
CREDIT SALES MANAGER

**Fig. 2.2**   Printout of completed form letter

attend for an interview, the time and date of interview, but probably not the venue, would also be different. These differences are known as *variables*.

On a typewriter you would have to type such a letter out ten times, and then type ten envelopes. On a word processor you key in the letter once, key in the variables ten different times and print out ten separate letters and envelopes, on the company's headed paper.

Remember that each machine will work in a slightly different way, but the principles of producing form letters are:

1   Key in the 'standard' letter, with the places where the variables occur marked by an asterisk or some other symbol.
2   Store this letter in the memory.
3   Re-call the letter to the screen and key in the variables for your first letter. Usually pressing a given key on the keyboard will enable you to jump straight to the space you need.
4   Print out the first letter and the envelope. (Note that on some systems all the variables for all the letters must be keyed in first, and then the printing out can take place. In this event, points 5 and 6 below would not apply.)
5   Re-call the standard letter to the screen, key in the variables for the second letter and print this out, with its envelope.
6   Continue in this way until all the letters are complete.

Whatever the system, the principle remains the same: the standard letter is keyed in only once. Variables are keyed in separately and the individual personal letters, with envelopes, are then printed out.

In an office, such as a Personnel Department, where letters of this kind are frequently sent out, then obviously the standard letter can be kept in the computer's memory, re-called for amendment and used whenever necessary.

**Mail merge**   The same principles apply here as for form letters – the standard letter is keyed in once, and the variables are keyed in separately. The difference is in the number of letters to be sent out, and the method used to merge the variables with the standard letter.

Perhaps your company wishes to advertise a product or a service by means of a mail shot to hundreds or thousands of potential customers. Before the coming of the word processor this meant a printed letter or duplicated letter with the name, address and salutation typed in or left out altogether.

With the word processor each letter can appear to be (and indeed is) addressed personally to the recipient. The recipient's name or address can be used in the text of the letter to make it even more personal, and the appearance of the letter will be that of a quality product. A 'personalised letter' is the result.

Mail merge is often a slightly more complicated process than form letter, and for this reason is used when large numbers of almost identical letters are required. In the case of mail merge the standard letter is keyed in; the names, addresses, salutations, etc., are keyed in *as a separate 'document'*; the two 'documents' are then *merged*.

Again, remember that different machines work in different ways, but for mail merge the principles are:

1 Key in the standard letter with the spaces for the variables indicated by (usually) a symbol and a number, for example:

    <1> = Name
    <2> = Address line 1
    <3> = Address line 2
    <4> = Address line 3
    <5> = Salutation

2 Store this standard letter in the memory.
3 Create a 'document' in which the variables – names, addresses, salutation, etc. – can be keyed in according to the precise format required by your particular machine. Names and addresses for this purpose are often acquired from telephone directories, trade publications, registers of electors, etc.
4 Key in the variables. This is very time-consuming.
5 Store the name and address list in the computer's memory.
6 Merge the two documents (the standard letter and the list of variables) together.
7 Print out each individual letter on the company's headed paper. This can occupy the printer for a considerable length of time.
8 Print out labels for the envelopes, or use window envelopes. When real bulk mailing is required, labels are much easier to print out than envelopes.

<1>
<2>
<3>
<4>
<5>

<6>

Dear <7>

**SPRING FLOWERS**

We have pleasure in enclosing our new Catalogue for our range of
spring bulbs.

We are sure that a discerning customer, such as yourself, will readily
appreciate the quality and variety of our range.  We would like to
draw your particular attention, however, to the **DUTCH HYACINTHS**
which we have made a speciality feature this year.

We look forward to your continued custom, and wish you well with your
autumn planting.

Yours sincerely


P L WARMING

Enclosure

**Fig. 2.3**  Mail merge letter with spaces for variables marked

# Warming's Garden Centre

Avery Corner

LARCHING

Hants

Mrs L R Huntley
'Marita'
29 Rushmore Close
LARCHING
Hants

5 August 1985

Dear Mrs Huntley

**SPRING FLOWERS**

We have pleasure in enclosing our new Catalogue for our range of
spring bulbs.

We are sure that a discerning customer, such as yourself, will readily
appreciate the quality and variety of our range.  We would like to
draw your particular attention, however, to the **DUTCH HYACINTHS**
which we have made a speciality feature this year.

We look forward to your continued custom, and wish you well with your
autumn planting.

Yours sincerely


P L WARMING

Enclosure

**Fig. 2.4**   Printout of completed mail merge letter

```
<><1>Mrs L R Huntley><2>'Marita'><3>29 Rushmore
Close><4>LARCHING>
<5>Hants><6>5 August 1985><7>Mrs Huntley>
<><1>Mr and Mrs G Sheffield><2>48 Burford
Road><3>Brockley><4>LARCHING><5>Hants><6>5 August 1985><7>Mr
and Mrs Sheffield>
<><1>The Revd R Smith><2>St Luke's Vicarage><3>Church
Road><4>WHITCHURCH><5>Hants><6>5 August 1985><7>Mr Smith>
<><1>J Browning Esq><2>7 Starts
Close><3>Locksbottom><4>ABBOTSLEIGH><5>Hants><6>5 August
1985><7>Mr Browning>
<><1>Captain D L Rockwell><2>'Uplands'><3>Bournemouth
Road><4>HINTON><5>Dorset><6>6 August 1985><7>Captain
Rockwell>
<><1>Mrs V Brightwell><2>12 Love
Lane><3>Fentdown><4>BOURNEMOUTH><5>Hants><6>6 August
1985><7>Mrs Brightwell>
<>
```

**Fig. 2.5**   Names and addresses keyed in ready for mail merge

For really large bulk mailing (say 5000 copies or more) then an agency or bureau which specialises in such work is sometimes used.

Whatever the method used to produce these 'personalised letters', the result is the same: a good-quality letter on the company's headed paper written and addressed, apparently personally, to the recipient.

If you are the recipient of such a letter, how do you tell whether it has been typed individually for you, or whether you are one among many? The method is not foolproof, but if you run your finger over the back of the letter, then on a manual typewriter or even sometimes on an electric one, you will feel where the fullstops have been typed in. Letters produced on electronic typewriters or word processors do not have these prominent fullstops!

## 2   Document compilation

This category, like the previous one, falls into two main sections: first, those documents, usually fairly lengthy, which in the main remain the same but need a considerable amount of variable information inserted into them, according to what is required at the time; second, those documents which are mainly made up of standard paragraphs or clauses brought together in a given order. The first has no specific name, but could be called an *insertion document*; the second uses a function called *boiler-plating* (welding various parts together to make a whole). Sometimes the two functions come together in one document.

**Insertion documents**    The sorts of documents which come into this category are contracts, property descriptions, administrative documents for calling meetings, joining instructions for training courses, and so on.

The main bulk of the document is set by law or custom, the documents themselves are used frequently or at regular intervals, but each time the variable information which is to be inserted is different.

Take, for example, a property description. In this case the format of the document, with its headings and any standard paragraphs or sentences are keyed in, with an asterisk or other symbol denoting the places where the variables are required, as in a form letter. The description of the various parts of the property is then added to the original format and the whole printed out to produce a master copy from which the required number of photocopies can be made.

In a contract between two parties, a contract of employment for example, then the majority of the document will be standard and can be stored in the computer's memory. It can be retrieved from the memory and the variables – employee's name, date of commencement of employment and other details relevant only to that employee – inserted, again as in a form letter.

**Boiler-plated documents**    Here the concept is rather different. A number of standard paragraphs are stored in the memory, each paragraph identified in some way – by a number, symbol or name. The person compiling the document will state which paragraphs are needed, and in which order. These paragraphs can then be retrieved from the memory as required and assembled to make a new document.

Many legal documents come into this category. A Will, for example, is made up of standard paragraphs, many of which will not vary from one Will to the next. In some parts of a Will, however, there may be two or more alternative paragraphs which could be used, in which case the one appropriate to the wishes of the Testator can be retrieved and boiler-plated in. Obviously there will then be variables which are different for every Will – the names of the

Testator, the Executors, the Beneficiaries, etc. – and these can be inserted as in a form letter.

Whatever the document required, the principle is the same – information which is standard and frequently required is stored in the memory; it is recalled as needed, boiler-plated together, and the variables inserted.

Of course, the content of the standard document must be agreed by all the people concerned, and this can sometimes be more of a problem than the actual compilation of the document. However, individual idiosyncracies of wording can always be inserted as variables!

## 3   Drafting

Many and varied are the documents which require several drafts before the final master copy can be printed out. It is not always because the author of the material is an inefficient or sloppy writer, but often because new information comes to light or the opinions of different people are sought. Examples of such documents are reports, bulletins, newsletters, literary drafts, specifications, scripts, minutes of meetings.

The beauty of the word processor is that insertions, deletions and corrections can be made easily. There are, however, hazards attached to this type of work which a little foresight can often avoid.

Take, for example, a lengthy report which has to be sent out within a fairly strict time limit. The first hazard is that the writer of the report, knowing that alterations can easily be made, makes the first draft more sloppy than necessary. Some companies have surveyed their output of such documents and have found that where three drafts were sufficient when typewriters were used, with word processors four or even five drafts are called for. Good drafting still saves time.

Amendments are usually necessary, however, and the discipline of clear amendments is just as important for word processing as it ever was for the typewriter. In addition, the way in which amendments are indicated sometimes needs to be different for the word processor. For example, the old 'cut and paste' method of amendment, where the writer would literally cut out a paragraph from one page and paste it onto another page, is no longer acceptable. If the

WP operator does not know from which part of the document a section has been removed, it will be extremely difficult to find that section, paragraph or sentence in order to move it. Therefore an alternative method of indicating the required move must be found. Phrases such as 'Take in A – A' are at least clear if well marked. The method by which the text is moved is sometimes called 'cut and paste' on the WP, but the writer must be discouraged from doing this literally.

Another hazard of drafts which need considerable amendment is that the operator will sometimes try to amend by using all the text editing facilities the word processor offers, when sometimes it would be more economical of time and effort to re-input the whole document. There can be no hard and fast rules for this. It is a matter of judgement and experience.

Of course, sections of the draft which are entirely correct do not need proof-reading a second time, and this can be very time saving. However, amendments which require proof-reading must be marked on subsequent drafts. Otherwise the temptation is to assume that, once amended, the document is totally correct, without further proof-reading.

Another minor calamity which can occur because only amendments are proof-read is that an amendment can sometimes make nonsense of another part of the document, or other parts are not themselves amended or re-numbered as necessary. If an entire document had to be re-typed, then the chances are that a good typist would find the anomaly, or re-number if required, simply because the whole text was being re-processed. Now, with a word processor, it is up to the author to make quite sure that amendments are followed through throughout the document.

So documents which require several drafts are a 'natural' for the WP, provided that amendments are indicated and processed in a disciplined way.

One further point about drafts which should be mentioned here, and which comes under the heading of disk management (see Chapter 7), is that it is very important to indicate in some way which draft is to be found on which disk under what name. It often occurs that the operator asked to amend a draft is not the operator who first keyed it in. The name given to the document (for example SCRIPT1) can be marked on the actual hard copy draft, and further

DRAFT                         (HOME AUTOMATION,
                                        `~ Imbolden`                          × ×

Was the zip fastener the first item of home automation?
Certainly it saves time; the two pieces of separate material can
be joined together in seconds.  It saves ⎰the laborious operation of  ×
fastening with hooks and eyes or buttons or safety pins.

And yet, we invariably exclaim over the exquisite workmanship of
the clothes of a past era when we have the opportunity of
examining them, especially ladies' gowns.  A zip in place of the
buttons and bows would undoubtedly spoil the aesthetic beauty of
such garments, though only a fraction of the time would be needed
to don them. ⎰⎺ Run  And so it is, it seems to me, with all manner of  ×
present-day items which technology has produced in the name of
progress to make our lives easier. ⎠ Run on                              ×

⎰
Invariably the new takes away something gracious from our lives.
   ∧ Take in Ⓐ - Ⓐ from next page                                      ×
A~~ few more examples come to mind and I am sure you could come up~~ ×
~~with others if you thought about it.~~  Take the smell of home
cooking.  What could be more delicious than the aroma of bacon
and eg̶ggs when you come in to breakfast from the garden on a   ×
lovely spring morning?  Or you come home fo̶rm work on a cold,  ×
wet, winter evening and open the door to the wonderful scents of
                Soup
so̶ap or meat simmering away on the cooker - or even better, on ×
the open fire.  But the micro wave oven does not produce those
mouth-watering smells.  It cooks so quickly the kitchen doesn't
get the chance to shimmer in the waves of apple dumpling smells,
so our anticipation of goodies to come is lost.  The innate
                                          disappear
reaction of salivation may, sadly, one day ~~be lost.~~             ×

**Fig. 2.6   An amended draft**

drafts (for example SCRIPT2) named and marked accordingly. (Hard copy is the WP term for the 'printed' page.)

Another important point to remember is that the first input of any long document (normally taken from manuscript or audio) is a long and often tedious business. This time – the time allowed for keying in – cannot be cut down. The word processor does not necessarily enable a 'typist' to key in more quickly – the time is saved at the amendments stage.

When it comes to printing out, remember a draft is what it says – a draft, and printouts need not necessarily be of top quality with carbon ribbon. In addition, they need not be on top quality paper, and the back of once-used computer paper (which is usually continuous stationery) gives a printout with plenty of space for writing in amendments. Do make sure, though, that no confidential information, particularly personal data which should not be disclosed, is on the printout.

## 4 Updating

Much has been said about amending drafts, but there are many documents in daily use which require amending in the sense of updating. Examples of these are price lists, car parking or telephone lists, employee records, catalogues, schedules, instruction manuals and so on. All these need to be up to date and will need amending, frequently or occasionally, to keep them so.

Again, the original keying in of the document will be no less time-consuming and entirely dependent upon the speed and accuracy of the operator. The updating, however, can be extremely rapid and save a great deal of time and frustration.

Take, for example, a list of internal telephone numbers as shown in Fig. 2.7.

Perhaps one person leaves and is replaced. Without a word processor the entire list would have to be re-typed. On the WP however, the sequence is:

1 Re-call the document from the computer's memory.
2 Delete the old name and insert the new one in the most efficient way for a particular machine.
3 Store the amended list in the computer's memory (the original is rarely required again).

INTERNAL TELEPHONE NUMBERS

| | | | | | |
|---|---|---|---|---|---|
| ABBOTT | Peter | 276 | HARRIS | Luke | 204 |
| ARJOON | Ali | 143 | HAYWARD | Virginia | 100 |
| ARROWSMITH | Rita | 273 | HEATH | Sylvia | 216 |
| ATKINS | John | 160 | HILLS | Steven | 154 |
| | | | HORTON | Kim | 228 |
| BAILEY | Susan | 158 | HUGHES | Winston | 147 |
| BATCOMBE | Bill | 123 | | | |
| BEALE | Colin | 246 | INMAN | Judith | 164 |
| BLACK | Karen | 267 | INWARD | Valerie | 222 |
| BROWN | Peter | 101 | | | |
| | | | JAMES | Cyril | 233 |
| CLARKE | Gerard | 126 | JENKINS | Alwyn | 193 |

**Fig. 2.7**   A document requiring occasional updating

4   Print out the revised list.
5   Copy the amendment onto any back-up disks held.
6   Photocopy the required number of copies.

The whole operation will probably not take more than five minutes, provided that the document can be quickly found and that a note has previously been made of the printstyle to be used. The disciplines needed to ensure this efficiency are described in detail in Chapter 7.

The list of telephone numbers is a very simple example of a document that needs updating. A procedure manual can be very complicated but the principles remain exactly the same:

1   Find the section or sections which need updating.
2   Make and proof-read the amendments.
3   Re-store the amended documents on disk, taking backup copies as necessary.
4   Print out and photocopy the required number of copies.

The secret is to be able to find the document, section, page and paragraph quickly and easily. Updating then becomes a very simple matter.

The four categories just examined – bulk mailing, document compilation, drafting and updating – have all been concerned with text in some way. The word processor can also be used to process figures to a certain extent.

## Processing figures and forms

### Figures

A figure is just as much a 'character' on the word processor as is a letter: 1, 2, 3, can be keyed in just as easily as a, b, c. A space is also counted as a character. Obviously, therefore, any tabulation work requiring columns of figures is no more or less possible than on a typewriter. The method used to achieve tabulation is different, and is explained in detail in Chapter 6, but the principles behind it are the same.

So WP can be used for balance sheets, timetables, investment portfolios and any document in which figures are involved. Some software programs allow the moving of whole columns of figures (called *column manipulation*). If, for example, figures for January to June were keyed in, and the information required was for six months, updated monthly, then at the end of July the figures for July could be keyed in and the January figures automatically dropped. As you can see, this is not so much processing the figures mathematically as manipulating characters on the screen – one of the basic WP functions.

Some processors do have a 'Maths Pack', or can go into 'Maths Mode', where simple arithmetical functions (adding, subtracting, multiplying, dividing) can be performed, but this is much more a mathematical function than true processing of data.

Yes, figures can be 'processed' on a word processor, but in a

EXPENDITURE

|  | JAN | FEB | MAR | APR | MAY | JUN |
|---|---|---|---|---|---|---|
| RENT |  |  |  |  |  | 550.00 |
| RATES |  | 125.00 |  |  | 125.00 |  |
| LIGHT/HEAT | 452.40 |  |  | 395.74 |  |  |
| REPAIRS | 25.36 | 26.98 |  | 115.14 | 48.72 |  |
| TELEPHONE |  |  | 138.29 |  |  |  |

**Fig. 2.8** Printout of a six-column tabulation

EXPENDITURE

| | FEB | MAR | APR | MAY | JUN | JUL |
|---|---|---|---|---|---|---|
| RENT | | | | | 550.00 | |
| RATES | 125.00 | | | 125.00 | | |
| LIGHT/HEAT | | | 395.74 | | | 236.87 |
| REPAIRS | 26.98 | | 115.14 | 48.72 | | 66.78 |
| TELEPHONE | | 138.29 | | | | 198.20 |

**Fig. 2.9** The tabulation updated. The January figures have been automatically dropped

rather limited way, either as characters being manipulated around the screen, or as figures subjected to simple mathematical processing. However, as mentioned in the previous chapter, word and data processing are becoming much more intertwined, and the line dividing them is often very fine indeed.

**Forms**

One thing the word processor is *not* good at is filling in forms which are not designed for a particular machine. Because all the text must first be keyed in and correctly positioned on the screen, it is difficult to get insertions in the right place on a pre-printed form. It *can* be done, but it takes time and is a fiddly process.

If certain forms are frequently required, then it is much better to design the form on the WP itself, store it in the computer's memory, recall it when necessary, fill in (or 'infill') the required information and print it out in its entirety. Examples of this are invoices, statements, etc. for small companies who still keep their books manually. Records of all kinds can be pre-designed on the WP and updated and printed out when required.

Many word processors have excellent facilities for form design, allowing the designer to create horizontal and vertical lines, to leave spaces and 'boxes' where required and to key in headings, etc. which can be 'protected' so that they are not accidentally deleted when the form is recalled to the screen for the input of fresh information.

Fig. 2.10 shows an example of an Invoice created on a word processor and used by a small company which has not yet computerised its book-keeping and accounts. The arrows indicate the protected areas or 'fields'.

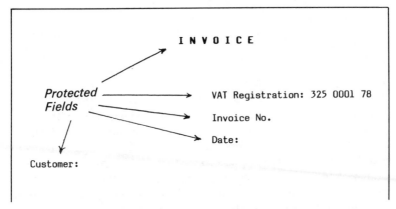

**Fig. 2.10**  A form designed on and for the word processor

It is also possible to design, and have pre-printed, forms which *will* match up with the word processor. In this case the screen format which fits the ultimate printout is established at the time of the form design. Then, each time a printout of that form is required, the format is called to the screen, the variable information keyed in, and the result is printed out on the pre-printed form.

## Basic and advanced WP functions and features

Several basic WP features and functions have been mentioned as the applications were described. The rest of this chapter sets out the features and functions in some detail.

Word processing software is developing so rapidly that it is almost impossible to say at any one moment which functions and features are basic, or standard (you would expect to find them on any machine), and which are more sophisticated or advanced. This depends partly on the memory capacity of the machine, and partly on the way in which the software program is written. Any line drawn between basic features and advanced features will, therefore, of necessity be arbitrary.

There are certain basic functions and features which one would expect to find with most self-respecting WP software programs. These, together with the more advanced features, are listed below under three main headings:

Input
Storage and Retrieval
Printing Out

## INPUT – basic functions

**The cursor**   This is one feature of a WP (and of most computers) which is well-nigh universal. A cursor is a small oblong or square which indicates whereabouts on the screen the operator is working. On some systems it appears below a character (a letter, figure or space), on some it 'covers' a character, on some it flashes, on some it does not (on some you may choose to have it flashing or not). It moves along as text is keyed in, or can be moved by the operator to the required position on the screen. The use of the cursor control keys is described in Chapter 5.

The word *cursor* comes from the latin verb 'currere', meaning 'to run': it 'runs' around the screen. The words cursory, cursive and courier come from the same root.

**Correcting text**   Sometimes, inevitably, mistakes are made when text is keyed in, and sometimes text requires amendment for various reasons. Correcting text is very easy on most word processors, and includes the following:

1   Correcting (often by 'overtyping') mis-keyed characters;
2   Deleting characters, words, phrases, sentences and paragraphs;
3   Inserting characters, words, phrases, sentences and paragraphs;
4   Deleting or inserting whole pages or sections of text.

**Moving text**   Any amount of text, from one character to whole sections, can normally be moved to a different place in the document. It can either be moved so that no part of it is left in the original place (this is often called 'cut and paste' or 'block move') or it can be repeated elsewhere in the document, the original being left where it is (this is often called 'cut and leave' or 'block copy').

Sometimes it is necessary to exchange pieces of text – two sentences or paragraphs, for example – but if you think logically about it, what you are actually doing is cutting, say, the second paragraph and pasting it above the first. The paragraphs seem to have changed places, but you have only moved one of them.

**Text alignment**   Obviously, if you have made corrections or amendments, or have been moving text within a document, then gaps are likely to occur. Pressing the right key or keys will re-align the text for you.

**Wraparound** On most systems when you are keying in and come to the end of a line, the text will automatically wrap itself round onto the next line – you do not have to press a 'carriage return' key. This means that you can carry on keying in without worrying about the right-hand margin, once it is set. The program will move the appropriate whole word to start the next line. On some machines a light or an audible 'bleep' might indicate the 'hot zone' (within, say, six characters of the right-hand margin), like the bell on a type-writer, but generally speaking this warning is not needed unless you have very long words which you would prefer to hyphenate.

**Hyphenation** There is usually a facility for you to tell the machine whether you wish hyphens at the end of lines to be used or to be ignored – hyphenated words are also transferred in total to the next line if the hyphens are ignored.

**Centring** Of course, you will often want to centre headings, lines or whole paragraphs. Usually pressing one or two keys will centre the chosen text between the given margins – it is no longer necessary to do this mathematically.

**Margins** Margins, on the other hand, do need to be set math-ematically, but left- and right-hand margins can be set very easily, and altered for a whole document or part of a document (even just one paragraph) with no difficulty at all.

**Tabs** Likewise, straight tabs can be set and altered at will. Most machines also have decimal tabs, centring tabs (for centring head-ings over columns, for example) and right-hand tabs. These latter enable text to be aligned to the right-hand margin, as in the example (see Fig. 2.11), and are not the same as right-hand justification of the text, which is described under the Printing Out section in this chapter.

```
101 High Street
       BROMLEY
          Kent
```

**Fig. 2.11** Text aligned to right-hand margin

**Inset text**   The names given to this facility vary considerably (temporary margin and auto tab are two such), but they mean the facility to return automatically to an inset portion of text (see Fig. 2.12) without having to return to the left-hand margin and tab across to the inset text each time.

xxxxxxxxxxxxxxxxxxxxxxxxxxxxxxx

xxxxxxxxxxxxxxxxxxxxxxxxxxxxxxx

        xxxxxxxxxxxxxxxxxx

        xxxxxxxxxxxxxxxxxx

        xxxxxxxxxxxxxxxxxx

*Margin automatically returns to here until told otherwise.*

**Fig. 2.12**

**Wide/landscape work – horizontal scrolling**   You will sometimes need to present work in landscape rather than portrait form (wider than the width of the screen, which is normally 80 characters wide). Most systems will allow you to do this and will automatically enable you to see what you have keyed in by scrolling your text on the screen from right to left. The left-hand portion of text seems to disappear into the left-hand side of the screen and the right-hand portion of the text is revealed as you key it in. A return to the left-hand margin will bring the left-hand portion back to the screen again. This is normally called *horizontal scrolling*.

**Vertical scrolling**   As text is keyed in beyond the normal number of lines on a screen (23), then the text will be automatically scrolled up and will seem to disappear into the top of the screen.

**Lower case and upper case**   Text is keyed in as on a normal typewriter, using the SHIFT keys for upper-case keys. On some systems it is possible to convert designated portions of text from lower to upper case or vice versa without re-keying the text.

**Search and replace**   This might, perhaps, be regarded as an 'advanced' function, as indeed might lower and upper case conversion.

Here commands can be given to search for a word (or combination of words) throughout the text and replace that word, wherever it is found, with a different word. For example, you might wish to replace the word 'company' with the word 'organisation' throughout the document. On some systems each instance of the word 'company' would be found and the operator would have to alter it to 'organisation'. On some systems the replacement would be done automatically (called *Global Search and Replace*).

**Form letters and mail merge**    These facilities have been described in some detail earlier in the chapter, and should be found on most word processing software programs.

### INPUT – advanced functions
Some companies have word processing software written for them, in which case any special needs would be taken into account and built into the software. There are, however, very many commercial WP software packages and programs which include what can be called advanced functions.

'Advanced' does not necessarily mean that the function is more difficult to operate, although sometimes this is the case. It usually means a function which takes up a lot of the computer's memory and one which is not used all the time. Described below are some of the more popular 'advanced' functions which may or may not be available with a given machine.

**Abbreviation files and strings**    If you have complicated words, or phrases which will be repeated many times within a document, then you can store these in the computer's memory identified by an abbreviation of the word or phrase required. Suppose, for example, you had a piece of work in which the words 'transcendental meditation' occurred frequently. You could store the phrase under 't m', or even just 't', and every time you wished to use the words then pressing the correct control key, followed by 't', would bring 'transcendental meditation' into the document.

**Background merging**    When performing the mail merge function, some systems will allow you to do the actual merging of the two documents 'in the background', so that you can be getting on with other work on the screen while the operation (which is often a very long one) is taking place.

**Boiler-plating**   This has been described earlier in the chapter and is the facility which allows you to 'weld' together in one document several paragraphs or pages stored separately in the computer's memory.

**Column manipulation**   This, too, has been described earlier, and is the facility which allows you to manipulate columns of figures or words around the screen – just as the name suggests.

**Double columns**   This is a very useful feature and allows you to create two (and sometimes three or more) quite independent columns of text on a page. Within each distinct column you can set margins and tabs, print out with the right-hand margin in *each* column justified, etc. It is most useful in documents such as news-letters, manuals, etc.

**Form design**   This, in a sense, can be done with any WP software, but there are some more sophisticated programs which help you design complicated forms, protecting headings so that they are not easily or accidentally deleted.

**Graphics**   Graphics facilities (the ability to draw lines, graphs, charts, etc.) are becoming more and more commonplace, and could perhaps be included under 'standard' features. However, on most true WP machines they are not universally included as a basic function.

**Maths pack**   As has been mentioned earlier, this facility enables the operator to do simple arithmetical calculations (addition, sub-traction, multiplication and division), including percentages, and can hold calculations in its memory – rather as an ordinary calcu-lator does.

**Scratch files**   These could well be called by another name such as the SAVE function or the RULER. They are portions of temporary or 'buffer' computer memory where one can store, temporarily, a limited amount of text and recall it to the screen at will. If you are doing tabulation work and require the headings to be repeated every now and again, then store them in the temporary memory or *scratch file* and recall them when required by pressing the appropriate key.

**Sorting** This facility enables you to sort lists of words or figures alphabetically or numerically. Sometimes it will perform a 'pure' sort in strict alphabetical order, but sometimes only into all the A's, all the B's, etc. Sometimes it will sort descending (Z to A or 100 to 1) as well as ascending (A to Z or 1 to 100). This is an example of a feature which requires fairly sophisticated software, but is usually quite easy to perform.

**Spelling** Basic spelling packages fall into two different categories. The first is where a given vocabulary (some of which may be compiled by the user of the system) is stored in the computer's memory, and every time a word is keyed in it is checked by the computer against the vocabulary in the memory and the computer will draw the operator's attention to any mis-spelling by a bleep or a flashing symbol or other device. The operator then has to check whether the spelling is correct and alter it if it is not. This type of spelling pack often cannot differentiate between homonyms (such as 'their' and 'there' or 'week' and 'weak'). It is very useful where scientific or very specialised and perhaps difficult vocabulary is needed.

The second is *particularly* useful for difficult vocabulary, and allows the operator to key in only the first, or perhaps the first two or three letters of a technical word (such as tetrahydrochloric – 'tet'), and the whole word will appear correctly on the screen – rather after the manner of an abbreviation file. Spelling packages can contain up to many thousands of words.

**Split screen** This is not the same as double-column work, but enables the operator to have two different sections of a document on the screen at the same time, perhaps for the purpose of comparison, and to operate each part of the screen independently.

**HELP!** This facility is coming more and more into usage and is mentioned here separately from the other features because it performs a slightly different function. It does not enable the operator to perform a specific function, but is there to help if the operator has got into a muddle, and this can happen quite frequently when learning the machine!

Pressing the HELP key will not normally tell you exactly what you have done wrong, but will call up a 'user-friendly' menu which suggests a variety of paths which you might follow to extricate yourself from the unfortunate position in which you find yourself.

### STORAGE – basic features and functions

The way in which work is stored in the computer's memory is described in the next chapter. Here the intention is to give an idea of the sorts of storage facilities available, irrespective of the size of the memory or of the disks used.

**Basic storage**   Most WP work will need to be stored for future use, for amendment, etc., and once keyed in it can be 'saved' on a 'work' or 'storage' disk. The text will normally remain stored on the disk until the operator wishes to do something else with it.

**Retrieval for amendment**   This is normally a very simple process of re-calling the work back from the disk where it is stored to the screen, where it can be further processed. The secret here is to be able to find the correct document in the first place.

**Catalogue/index**   Most systems will allow the operator to find out what is on a disk by throwing up on the screen and/or printing out a catalogue or index of the work stored on that particular disk. Sometimes the catalogue is in alphabetical order. Sometimes it is in the order in which the work was stored on the disk. It will normally indicate the length of the piece of work stored and, of course, its name and description.

**Document naming and re-naming**   Most systems require the operator to name a piece of work (which is usually called a document). There is also a facility for describing the document and dating it for easy identification in the catalogue/index. There is usually, too, a facility for varying the name of the document, or re-naming it entirely, if required.

**Disk space remaining**   The system will normally tell the operator how much space remains on the disk being used. This is normally expressed as a percentage, but could be either the amount of work already on the disk (Disk 37% full) or the amount of space left on the disk (63% remaining).

**Security**   Security is a very important part of word processing and most systems have some very basic security facilities. This may only go as far as the protection of documents so that they cannot be deleted accidentally. The simplest form of security is to make certain that the disks containing sensitive information are locked away, together with any copies which may exist, until they are needed.

## STORAGE – advanced functions

As with input, the line which can be drawn between basic and advanced storage functions is necessarily arbitrary. The functions described here may be found with some simple WP software, but usually they appear with a more sophisticated software package.

**Catalogue/index information**   As well as the information fed in to the machine by the operator – the document name and description, and the date, if required – a more advanced system may show in the catalogue/index additional information such as the time of original input, the date and the time of amendments, the length of the document in keystrokes/characters and the speed of input by the operator. Again this information can be called to the screen or printed out, as needed.

**Automatic deletion**   One of the disciplines which word processing imposes is the need to delete unwanted documents at a given time if disks are not to be cluttered up with unwanted information. Some systems allow this to be done automatically after expiry of the time indicated by the operator.

**Reclaim disk space**   When documents are deleted from a disk, because of the way in which information is stored (explained more fully in the next chapter) then sometimes wasted storage space remains unusable on the disk until the system is given the command to reclaim that space. On a fairly full disk the amount of space reclaimed may be no more than one or two percent, but it can be useful and might make all the difference between having to start a new disk or not.

**Automatic duplication**   Duplication of disks is an essential discipline in word processing and this subject is discussed more fully in

Chapter 7. Suffice it to say here that some systems will automatically make a copy of any work stored on the disks.

**Security**   For really sensitive material various security devices exist to minimise the possibility of information being deleted or tampered with. These generally mean that only designated personnel may have access to the information through a series of codes or passwords. Sometimes the password will appear on the screen when keyed in, and sometimes not. Some systems will allow an operator to have access to information, but not to alter or amend it in any way. The requirement for sophisticated security devices will depend very much, of course, on the nature of the business and who needs to know what.

### PRINTING OUT – basic features and functions
The various types of printer are described in the next chapter, and the printout facilities available will depend not only on how the WP software is written, but also on the type of printer used. The printout facilities described in this chapter do not differentiate between the types of printer.

**Print pitches**   The *pitch* is the size of typeface (not its style) available on the WP. The sizes normally available are 10, 12 and 15 (ten, twelve and fifteen characters to the inch, the last of these being the smallest). Proportional spacing (when the characters are given a space in proportion to their width – for example, 'i' will take up less space than 'm') is also widely available.

**Print styles**   There is a very wide range of print styles. The important thing is to check that the style you want is available for your particular printer, and also that it is available for metal or plastic daisy wheels, if that is the type of printer used. There are normally charts showing the different styles available for a given printer.

**Changing print pitches or styles**   Many systems allow you to interrupt a print run in order to change the size or style of the print (sometimes called a *font*) in the middle of a document.

**Interrupt or abort print**   The changing of the size or style of print presupposes that a print run can be interrupted. Most systems will allow you to do this and to abort, or stop, the print run altogether should you need to do so.

**Right-hand justification**  Almost all systems have this printout facility. It means that the right-hand margin as well as the left-hand margin is 'justified', in other words is even all the way down the page (like the text of this book). The words along a line are automatically spread out so that the right effect is achieved. Some systems justify everything until told not to do so.

**Line spacing**  Most systems can produce single, double and treble line spacing. Not all can produce 1½ and 2½. Normally the line spacing on the screen will appear single, even though the printout, given the right commands, might be double or another variation. It is also normally possible to vary the line spacing within a document. What is *not* easy to do is to squeeze in an extra line by turning up the line spacer on the printer a little, as you can on a typewriter. It is possible to interrupt the print run and turn the paper up or down a little in the printer, but it is very difficult to get it accurate and is usually not worth the time and trouble it takes.

**Pagination**  This means, in a lengthy document, breaking the document into pages often after a given number of lines per page – usually between 55 and 60 for an A4 sheet of paper. Once the pagination print command has been given, the document will be broken into pages automatically throughout, taking no account of the sense of what is said, or of paragraphs. It is necessary, therefore, to be able to override the pagination print command for individual pages when the paragraphing matters, and this facility is normally available.

**Page numbering**  Obviously each page of a document can be numbered when the operator is keying in the text, and for short documents of only a few pages this is easy to do – sometimes easier than commanding the machine to number the pages automatically.

Automatic page numbering might be considered to be an advanced feature, rather than a standard, basic feature, but it is fairly common and thus appears under this heading. It enables the operator to dictate at which page the numbering should start (introductory and contents pages are often not numbered, so the numbering starts on the third or fourth page) and which number (1, 2, 3, etc.) shall appear on the first numbered page. The correct page number is then printed out automatically for every page of the document. This is particularly useful when a long document has fresh pages inserted – it means that when re-printed, all the pages will automatically be re-numbered. It does mean that a completely fresh printout is required, but this is a great deal less irritating than having to re-type a complete document.

**Headers and footers**   Headers and footers are lines of text (such as a heading) which need to be repeated on every page. Page numbering is one such example and can appear at the top of the page or the bottom, to the left or the right or in the middle of the page, as desired. Most systems allow two headers and footers (two lines in all, not two headers and two footers) and will permit the operator to say whereabouts on the page they should appear.

**Number of copies**   A lot of word processing work requires one master copy from which photocopies are made. However, there are times when several printouts of a document are required, and most systems can easily cater for the number of copies needed.

**Single or continuous printing**   This means that documents can be printed out page by page, with the printer stopping at the end of every page, or continuously, without stopping. Which the operator chooses depends, of course, on the nature of the work being printed out and the type of stationery being used.

**Methods of emphasis – emboldening and underlining**   Emboldening means that when being printed out, the emboldened words are struck, very rapidly, twice instead of once, and slightly out of synch, and thus appear darker on the paper. Underlining is what it says – the words chosen by the operator are underlined. As in typewriting, this facility is also used to 'draw' horizontal lines across a page.

Emboldening and underlining appear here, rather than in the Input section, because it is only when printing takes place that the method of emphasis chosen becomes apparent. Sometimes the designated words, headings, etc., appear emboldened or underlined on the screen, but very often they do not – although emboldened or underlined words are always indicated in *some* way. It is when the *keying in* is being done that the emboldening or underlining must be done by the operator, but it is in the *printing out* that the results appear.

**PRINTING OUT – advanced features**
**Methods of emphasis – emboldening and underlining**  There are some additional emboldening and underlining features on some systems. These include:

1  Semi-emboldening (emboldened words are struck three times, semi-emboldened ones twice).
2  Double underlining.
3  Printing white within black instead of black on white.

**Printing from screen**  Printing out is normally done once the work has been stored on disk. It is possible on some systems, however, to print out either the whole of what is on the screen at the time, or part of it. This can be very useful for printing out a whole page which you do not wish thereafter to keep.

**Background printing**  This generally means that one document can be printed out while another one is being keyed in or amended on the screen.

**Specialised work**  Most simple systems cannot deal with highly specialised mathematical, scientific or technical work. The print-wheels do not have the symbols needed to accomplish this. With special software, keyboard and printwheels, it is possible to undertake very specialised work. Many printwheel charts will show that printwheels are available in different languages – Greek, Arabic, etc. – and these will print out perfectly well *if* the special software is available to go with them. The software has to tell the machine which letter on the keyboard represents a Greek Π or Δ for example.

More general European accents (for example, the acute and grave accents and circumflex in French, and the umlaut in German) are fairly commonly available, and it is a question of identifying which key on the keyboard corresponds to the character on the printwheel. The £ sign often does not appear marked on an American keyboard, and has to be identified. Some printwheels do not have the £ sign – some do not have even common fractions (¼, ½, ¾). It is always worth checking *before* using a particular printwheel.

**Print queues**  When several terminals (screens and keyboards) are sharing a printer – and it is perfectly possible for about six terminals to share one printer, although not necessarily an economic proposition – then a print 'queue' is formed. The printer will automatically take the documents in turn as the command to print them is given. Print queues are a normal feature of shared logic systems (see page 61).

Advanced systems will allow an operator or supervisor to override the print queue for urgent documents. Problems which arise here are usually more to do with man management than machine management.

**Print selections**   Sometimes it is necessary to print out only part of, say, a list of names and addresses. Suppose, for example, a company had sent out a large mail shot to firms all over the UK, but wanted to do a follow up for those firms based in London. Given the right commands, the printer could print out labels or letters for only those firms who had 'London' on a specific line of the address. This line must be specified at the time of keying in. In other words, the system can *select* and print out the designated parts of a list.

As can be seen, word processing can 'do' a lot of things. When choosing a WP system it is very important to decide exactly which functions and facilities are essential to you, and which are desirable, and to select the software and hardware accordingly. Hardware and software are described in the next chapter.

# 3

# How Does Word Processing Work?

A word processor is a computer, and as such has all the attributes and components of a computer. It is not the intention of this chapter to describe how a computer works internally, but rather to enumerate the various parts which make up the computer/word processor which are necessary for it to work.

## Hardware

Hardware is the general term used to cover all the tangible parts of the system – if you can touch it, it is hardware; if not, it is software (see page 57). The term does not normally include accessories and stationery, such as disks and printwheels, but is applied more properly to the parts which make up the computer itself.

The design of each system varies considerably, for economic, ergonomic, capacity and aesthetic reasons. Within each system, however, are certain basic components.

### 1 Central processing unit (CPU)

This is the 'power house' of the computer, and is made up of two parts, the *arithmetic unit* and the *control unit*.

The arithmetic unit is a mechanism capable of performing simple calculations at very high speed, and the control unit 'controls' the operation of the computer to ensure that each unit is synchronised.

### 2 Memory

There are two types of *memory*: the first, called *fast store*, is used to store data temporarily and is usually combined with, but is not part of, the CPU. It is more often called the RAM (random access memory), and specifications for computer/word processors will usually quote the RAM capacity of the system – e.g. 132K of RAM. What this means is described more fully under the Software section of this chapter.

RAM memory is volatile, and disappears when the word processor is switched off, hence the need for a more permanent type of memory. This is called *backing store*, and is used for storing the work you put on the word processor. There are many backing store devices (such as disks, tapes and cassettes), which are more fully described in the Storage Media section of this chapter.

### 3   Peripherals

Pieces of equipment which are added or built in to the system to enable people to use it are called *peripherals* – these are divided mainly into *input* devices and *output* devices. Input devices allow the user to put data in to the computer, and output devices receive information from the computer and transmit it in a form which is understandable to the user.

**Input devices – the keyboard**   Input devices range from punched tape and card readers through keyboards to voice input and optical character readers (OCRs). An OCR machine 'reads' pages of typescript directly into the word processor, and a WP operator can often use this machine to input text instead of keying it in through the keyboard. Some OCR machines can read any print style or font, but many can read only specific fonts, so that not all typescript can be used on the OCR. The most common input device for the word processor, however, is the QWERTY keyboard, and this is the device which it is presumed most WP operators will use.

The layout of the keyboard is much the same as it has been for many years now, as far as the alphabetical characters are concerned. The difference on a word processor is that an additional range of editing and function keys is needed on most systems, and the layout of these varies from system to system.

Fig. 3.1 shows a typical word processor keyboard.

The keyboard is often attached to the screen by a cable, instead of being fixed, so that it can be moved to different positions on the desk to suit the operator. It is also possible to use different keyboards

**Fig. 3.1** Keyboard with alphanumeric, function and editing keys

with the same screen, by unplugging the keyboard and plugging in a different one (with a pad of numerals, for example).

Word processing keyboards tend to be flatter than typewriter keyboards, creating a different angle for the positioning of the hands. They all have a very light touch – lighter than an electric typewriter – and are very much quieter than typewriter keyboards.

The shape of the keys themselves can vary from system to system. Some are so flat that they are uncomfortable for many users, as there is no feeling of resistance when the key is pressed. Generally speaking, however, they are quite comfortable to use. Once you have become accustomed to an electronic keyboard a normal typewriter keyboard, particularly a manual one, feels very heavy indeed.

Because the touch is so light, the keys tend to 'run away with you', and you make more mistakes than you would normally do. Mistakes on a word processor are very easy to correct, however, and the work is only on the screen at this stage, not on paper, so the situation is not nearly so traumatic as it might appear.

Setting your hands on an electronic keyboard for the first time can be alarming, but once you realise that you will find it very difficult to damage the machine or someone else's work, then the fear is soon dispelled.

**Input devices – the screen**    In a sense a screen is an input device, particularly if it is a touch-sensitive screen where you only have to touch a given part of the screen to move text or delete it, etc. A screen is more normally regarded as an output device, however, because it shows to the user the data which has been input via the keyboard.

**Output devices – the screen** The screen is a most important peripheral and is usually attached to the keyboard in some way. Screens are often called VDUs (Visual Display Units) and sometimes CRTs (Cathode Ray Tubes), as in a television set.

Fig. 3.2 shows a typical VDU with movable keyboard. The two together are referred to as a *terminal*.

Screens are usually rectangular, and can display 80 characters across and 23 lines down. There are larger screens which can display

**Fig. 3.2** Screen and keyboard making a terminal

a whole page of A4, and smaller screens which can only display correspondingly fewer lines and/or columns.

They are usually housed in attractive plastic casings which can tilt and swivel to suit the operator. Some sit squarely on the desk top, others are on small 'pedestals'. It is very much a matter of taste which to choose – the most important thing is that the whole terminal should be comfortable and efficient to use.

One thing which *will* determine the comfort of the screen is its colour. Some show white on black, or grey; some show green on black; some black on white like paper; some yellow on brown. It is normally a little time, unfortunately, before an operator can be sure which colour is the most comfortable to use for long word-processing sessions, which makes the choice of colour in the first place difficult. Some systems offer a choice of colour.

Most systems have a brightness control which enables the oper-

**Fig. 3.3**  Switches and screen controls

ator to adjust the brightness of the screen, which can be important to some. The flicker – the apparent 'flickering' of the screen – can be a problem for some people and it is as well to opt for a screen which has a good, steady image which will suit most users. A dark casing round the screen itself helps to prevent glare from artificial light. The effects of the environment and the screen on an operator are more fully discussed in the next chapter.

Switches and screen controls are usually discreetly set in the plastic covering, often at the side or back of the terminal. Fig. 3.3 shows another screen with its controls.

**Output devices – the printer**   There are various types of printer available for WP systems. Because the quality of the work produced is of the highest importance, you should choose the best you are able to afford.

The most common are the *dot matrix* and *daisy wheel* printers. More sophisticated, more expensive and less common, particularly on a small system, are *ink jet* and *laser beam* printers.

The matrix printer forms dots using a series of needles. The greater the number of needles in the print head the denser (clearer) the character. However, the printout from these printers is not of first class quality, and is the sort of print you usually find on conventional computer printouts, where the quality of the print is not of such great importance. Recent dot matrix printers have the dots much closer together, so that the quality of the printout is greatly improved. Fig. 3.4 shows how characters are formed by a dot matrix printer.

Ink jet printers throw tiny jets of ink very quickly onto the paper; the quality is good and the speed fast. Even better and faster is the laser beam printer, which can handle large quantities of paper at very high speeds where the printout is of top-class quality.

The most common printer for word processing is the daisy wheel printer, and it is on this type of printer that this book will concentrate. Daisy wheels have characters on the end of each 'petal'. The wheel is spun very quickly by the printer and the hammer strikes the character required through a ribbon, very much in the manner of a typewriter. Fig. 3.5 shows a daisy wheel.

Daisy wheel printers come in various sizes and models. The best print out at a speed around 600 words a minute (or 45 characters per

**Fig. 3.4** The formation of characters on a dot matrix printer

**Fig. 3.5** A daisy wheel

second) and are often bi-directional: they print from left to right followed by right to left on the next line. The speed of the printer is often given in characters per second and ranges from 45 cps as mentioned above to 17 cps for electronic typewriters interfaced with a WP.

The speed of the best printers is impressive, but you have to remember that the time spent keying in and formatting, as well as printing, is the time which must be measured to obtain a true picture of the speed and efficiency of word processing.

These printers measure about 22″ wide × 18″ deep × 8″ high, and are attractively presented to match the rest of the hardware in the system. Fig. 3.6 shows a typical daisy wheel printer, with the familiar features, such as the paper release, the platten and the bail bar you would expect to find on a typewriter.

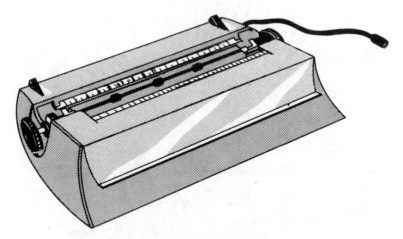

**Fig. 3.6**   A typical daisy wheel printer

Some printers also have warning lights on the front or the side to indicate whether the printer is on or off, and whether the ribbon and/or paper have run out. In some cases the printer just stops, and you have to guess whether it is out of paper or ribbon.

A printer is a fairly expensive peripheral, but one which a word processing system cannot do without.

**Input/output devices** The main input/output devices for a word processing system are, therefore, the keyboard, screen and printer. Input/output is often referred to as I/O, and if a screen message appears saying I/O ERROR, then it is sometimes an indication that there is a fault in one of these – usually the printer, which has moving parts. An I/O error can also be an error in the actual input (keying in) or output rather than in the I/O device itself.

**Disk drives** Another device essential to the working of the word processor is the *disk drive* (or cassette drive if cassette is the storage medium used). The disk drive for floppy disks usually has two slots, which can be horizontal or vertical, into which the disks are inserted. The drive then spins the disk round inside its black floppy casing and the heads on the disk drive read the information on the disk.

Disk drives for the larger, cartridge disks work in much the same way, but of course the disk drives themselves are larger and usually housed in a separate unit.

Floppy disk drives can be in a separate unit, or can be incorporated in the terminal. Figs. 3.7*a* and 3.7*b* show two different types of disk drive, the first in a self-standing desk top unit, the second integrated with the terminal.

Some very small systems have a single disk drive where only one disk at a time can be used. This does limit the capacity of the system to store information and makes disk copying well-nigh impossible. Most systems have a dual disk drive which makes for greater flexibility of disk use and greater capacity on the storage disks.

**Cables** Strictly speaking, cables might be described as accessories rather than hardware, but since the hardware will not work without the cables, they are included in this section. Cables not only connect the system to the power supply, they also connect the various peripherals to the CPU (one from the printer to the CPU, and one from the disk drive, if it is a separate unit, to the CPU). The length of the cables will, naturally, determine the positioning of the various pieces of hardware, and some of the cables are quite short.

Fig. 3.8 shows a typical configuration for a word processing system: the keyboard, VDU, printer, disk drive and cable – the minimum hardware needed to make word processing work.

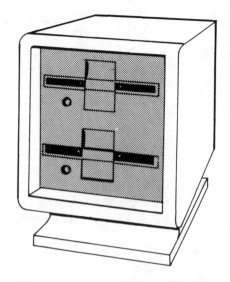

**Fig. 3.7a**   A self-standing disk drive

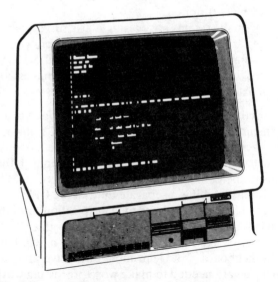

**Fig. 3.7b**   A disk drive integrated with the terminal

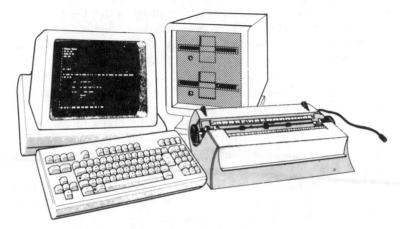

**Fig. 3.8** A typical word processing configuration

## Software

The hardware of the computer is merely machinery, and the computer has to be told what to do – it has to have a set of instructions known as a *computer program*. Programs, singly or collectively, are called *software*.

Hardware is no use without software. Conversely, software is no use without the hardware on which to run it. The two together go to make up the computer, but in the end the software and its quality are really more important than the hardware. You can buy expensive, attractive hardware with plenty of power and capacity, but without good, well-written software, which does what you want it to do, the hardware is of little consequence.

If the software is the set of instructions to make the hardware work, who writes the software, how is it written and how is it used on the computer? It is not the intention in this book to go into great detail on this, but an outline of how software works should be useful.

### Machine codes and computer languages

Software is written by a computer programmer, who knows what instructions are needed to make word processing work, and is capable of writing the program in a language which the computer can understand. Computers can only understand digitised numbers, that is a series of noughts and ones. There are special combinations of noughts and ones for each letter of the alphabet and other signs and symbols such as commas, percentage signs, etc. The combination of noughts and ones is called a *machine code*, which the computer *can* understand. It will recognise the letter 'a' in a popular American machine code called ASCII (pronounced 'Askey' – American Standard Code for Information Interchange) when it is translated into *binary arithmetic* (digitised) as 01100001. A capital 'A' is recognised when it is translated into binary as 01000001.

These noughts and ones are called BInary digiTS or *bits*, and a *byte* (by eight) is a combination of eight bits. One byte is normally considered equivalent to one character.

It is possible, although difficult, to write computer programs in machine code, but other languages, more like ordinary English, have been devised. The programmer can write in a 'normal' computer language which is then 'translated' into a machine code which the computer can understand. This *translator* or *interpreter* is another piece of software written for the purpose.

There are several *computer languages*, the most widely known of which is BASIC (Beginners All-purpose Symbolic Instruction Code) and is suitable for most applications. For some tasks a more precise computer language is required – programmers in commercial work, for instance, use COBOL (COmmon Business Orientated Language); FORTRAN (FORmula TRANslator) is used for scientific work.

### How software is used

All systems must have an important piece of software called the *operating system* (OS). This consists of a program which tells the computer how to control other programs, how to link in with the printer, etc. The operating system can be looked upon as the link between the hardware and the software, and is usually incorporated in the machine as a ROM (read only memory) micro chip. Two of the most common operating systems are DOS (pronounced 'doss') and CP/M, which are widely used on small systems.

As well as the operating system, each computer needs special software for the different applications – word processing, account-ing, etc. This is called *applications software*.

In order to use software on the computer, it must be in the fast store or RAM, and this is what is happening when the program is being *loaded* – it is being placed in the RAM from the disk. All data to be processed must also be in the RAM, so the size of the RAM is important.

The amount of RAM is measured by the term K, which is equivalent to 1024 binary characters, or bytes; this is usually simplified so that K is rounded to equal 1000 bytes (Kilobytes).

The very small computers might have 8K of RAM, slightly larger ones 16K, then 32K, 64K, etc., but it is important to remember that the RAM has to include the operating system, the applications software and then enough space to process any data fed in to the computer.

For example, in a 16K RAM system 5K might be taken up by the operating system and 7K by the word processing software, leaving only 4K (or six pages of A4 text) for the user. Graphics software can use as much as 8K to 20K of memory on its own, so that even on machines of 32K or 64K capacity, the amount of space left for the user is substantially diminished. So although the size of the memory is important, it is equally important to know how much of that memory is free to be used for inputting and processing data.

The amount of RAM space that can be accommodated on one micro chip in the CPU is increasing all the time as the technology continues to improve, so that 256K RAM systems should be widely available in small computers in the fairly near future at not too prohibitive a cost.

**The quality of the applications software**
The way in which applications software, word processing software for instance, is written will determine how easy or difficult it is to use. The programmer could use technical language instead of normal English when writing screen messages: SYNTAX ERROR, for example, means that you have made a keying in error, and could be more understandably expressed as CHECK KEYING.

Most WP programs are now 'user friendly', but some can require the operator to use very complicated codes or encoded commands to make the system work.

Similarly, if certain very common WP functions, such as emboldening, are 'extremely complicated to perform, then you might consider that the software for that particular function was badly written.

It is not easy to determine the quality of word processing software for yourself until you have used it for some time. Measures of its success can be how long it has been around, how well it has been tested and how widespread is its use.

Talking to other people who have used the same software can also be useful, although what is 'user friendly' to one person is not necessarily 'friendly' to another.

When considering software, therefore, remember to check the capacity *and makeup* of the RAM (how much is left free to the user) and the quality, if possible, of the applications software. Sufficient user space combined with good software leads to efficient and satisfying word processing.

## Configurations

This is the term used to describe the whole hardware set-up of the system. It will include the numbers of terminals, printers, disk drives, etc., which, when connected up, will be 'the system'. The size of the configuration will depend upon the size and type of system; for example, whether the computer is mainframe, a mini or a micro and whether it is shared logic, stand alone or networked. These are all terms which describe what size the computer is and whether it can work on its own or is linked up in some way.

### Mainframes, minis and micros

These terms all describe the size, method of operation and capacity of the computer.

A *mainframe* is normally a powerful, large computer used in large businesses or other organisations. It can be used for all sorts of computer applications, such as payroll, sales records and forecasts, stock records, data analysis, ordering procedures, book-keeping and accountancy all at the same time. It can also, if required, run a word processing package so that people in the organisation who need to use word processing can 'log on' through their own terminals to the main computer and use its power and capacity for their WP requirements. In this case the disk drives would be housed with the main computer, and the WP operator would only have the screen, keyboard and printer. The power of a mainframe computer can be useful but the response time (the time it takes for your screen to 'respond' to any commands given through the keyboard) can be slow, and the WP software package is often cumbersome and difficult to use.

*Mini* computers are smaller versions of mainframes and can often use data processing and word processing facilities simultaneously, but to a more limited degree. They would have several terminals, but not as many as on the mainframe, attached to the CPU, so that the disk drive would again be with the CPU and the workstation would have a keyboard, screen and access to a printer.

*Micro* computers are smaller still and usually consist of a desk-top CPU with disk drives, screen, keyboard and printer. Many are capable of using WP packages as well as, say, book-keeping and accounting packages, but·*not* simultaneously.

So, mainframe, mini and micro describe the size of the computer, not so much according to its actual physical size, but more related to its power and the capacity it has to perform many things at one time – or not. There is no hard and fast rule which says that a mainframe must be of a certain memory size before it can be called a mainframe, and similarly with the minis and micros, so that the terms are only an *indication* of size rather than an exact measurement.

Word processing on a mainframe has already been described. Word processing on minis and micros can also work in the same way, in other words as one software package to be used among many. Word processing is, however, such an essential part of many a large company's support services, that they use machines which are *dedicated* only to WP.

**Dedicated word processors**
These machines are used exclusively for word processing and often cannot be used for any other sort of computing. They can vary in size, just like any other system, and their configuration will vary accordingly.

Dedicated word processors can work on a *shared logic* system. This is normally mini computer size and consists of a CPU and several (up to about sixteen) terminals. Each terminal shares with the others the logic in the CPU, hence the name, and also stores the software program, so that once the software has been loaded at start of business, it is there for all to use throughout the day. These systems work mostly on hard disk, sometimes with the floppy disk alternative in the same system. Each workstation will have its own screen and keyboard, but a printer could be shared by two or three terminals. This sort of system – shared logic, dedicated almost exclusively to WP – is used by companies with a very large WP requirement, such as firms of solicitors.

Dedicated machines can be smaller and stand on their own – these are usually called *standalone* systems. Here, each workstation is on its own with its VDU, keyboard, disk drive and printer, and normally works on floppy disks. Its software program, like that of the shared logic system dedicated to WP, will be good, fast and easy to use. The system itself will be, probably, rather bigger than a desk-top micro, but not as big as a mini computer. It may have the facility to use other programs, such as accounts, but its main purpose will be WP, and it will be largely dedicated to that function.

**Desk-top micros and personal computers (PCs) as word processors**
These are usually small but versatile systems, word processing being only one of many software packages used on the one machine. Most of the WP packages used on this size of machine are perfectly adequate for the occasional WP user (for whom they are designed), but might prove tiresome to someone whose whole day is likely to be spent on word processing: they often do not have the power and the versatility to perform complicated WP functions as quickly as a dedicated WP. For personal and home use and for very small companies whose WP requirement is very limited, they are ideal, provided that the printer is of sufficiently high quality for the work involved. Naturally the configuration will be a single screen with keyboard, disk drive often integrated, and printer.

**Word processing on networks**
Networks are really an extension of the size, capacity and versatility of the mainframe computer. On a network, used in very large companies or in a particular geographical area by several smaller companies, each terminal can 'access' several different functions as

and when required. There is normally a large database of information which can be called up at will. There will often be electronic mail and message facilities and diary facilities where the 'diaries' of several people can be called up, compared and synchronised. There is normally, too, a WP package which in turn can get into (or access) the centrally stored files and documents, call the information to the screen and incorporate it as necessary in the work being done. This is where WP really extends itself into the main world of computers and information processing, as mentioned in Chapter 1, although this is true in a minor way of mini and micro computers as well. Here the configuration will be a powerful CPU with attendant disk drives and data storage facilities, and a network of terminals and printers connected to it.

So word processing can work on many different types and sizes of computer – the configuration will vary according to the size and requirements of the user. For people starting out in the WP world, or teaching themselves, the most likely configuration will be one terminal (screen and keyboard), a dual disk drive and a printer, with the necessary cables.

## Compatibility

One of the most irritating things about word processors is their incompatibility. Work done on one system cannot, generally speaking, be fed directly into another system. There are agencies which will convert work done on one system to another system and *interfaces* (specially constructed boxes or cables) which will enable the computers to *talk* to each other, but it is rarely as simple as taking a disk from one system, putting it into another and expecting it to work.

One of the things which is helping systems move towards compatibility is the common operating system, such as DOS or CP/M mentioned in the Software section. If you buy hardware which runs DOS or CP/M, then the range of applications software available to you is quite extensive.

This still does not mean that you can store work on your disk, take your disk to someone else's system and use your disk on the other system. Each new disk that you use has to be 'initialized' or 'formatted', which means that the new disk has to be 'prepared' in order to work on your system. The new disk has to receive operating instructions from the disk containing your system's software, so that when you key in work and store it on the new disk, it knows how to handle the commands you give it and will work on your hardware. You can then use your disk on your own hardware or on compatible hardware and software – that is, a system using the same hardware and software as your own.

For example, disks initialized and used on one personal computer should work on another personal computer of the same make and size. They are unlikely to work on a personal computer of a different make. They might work on a *larger* computer of the *same* make, but this is not always so. The disk sizes could be different, for one thing.

In addition to the initialized disks not being interchangeable between systems, the CPU will not always accept every peripheral you might wish to use. Your CPU might not, for example, work with every type of printer. Further still, the actual printwheel might not work on every printer with all WP applications software, and in that sense is incompatible.

Incompatibility *is* a problem, and you need to check that any pieces of machinery and equipment which you wish to use are compatible with each other, *and* with any other system you need to communicate with. Different systems in the same small office can cause distressing communication problems.

## Storage media

Word processing work can be stored on floppy or hard disks or on cassette tape. In addition, magnetic tape storage is often used on large, mainframe systems. Fig. 3.9 shows the different types of storage media available.

The most common storage media for word processing are floppy disks (sometimes called diskettes) and, on somewhat larger systems, hard, or cartridge or rigid disks – all three names mean the same thing. Some small systems use cassette tapes, but these are very slow, because you have to run the tape backwards and forwards to the appropriate point to find the work you want – using a disk, the finding of the work is random and well-nigh instantaneous. This book, therefore, will concentrate on the use of disks and diskettes as storage media.

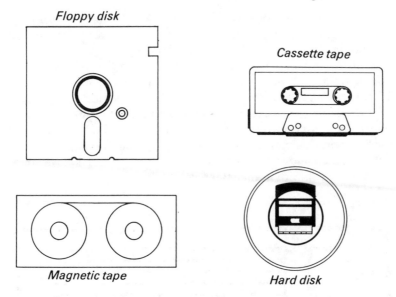

**Fig. 3.9** Storage media

**Floppy disks and diskettes – (sometimes called flexible disks)**
Floppy disks come in three main sizes: 8″, 5¼″ and 3½″. Naturally, you have to have the size which fits your disk drive. The disks can be:

*Single-sided*   Data is recorded on one side only and is used in single-head disk drives.

*Reversible*   Again for use on single-head disk drives. Data can be recorded on both sides of the disk, but the disk must be turned over by the operator when one side is full.

*Dual-sided*   For use on dual-head disk drives. The data is recorded on both sides of the disk.

*Single or double or quad density*   This refers to the density at which the bytes are recorded on each sector of the disk. The greater the density, the greater the storage capacity.

So the amount of work which can be stored on a disk varies considerably according to the disk size, whether it is single- or dual-sided, and its density. A typical 5¼″ dual-sided double-density disk will store, very roughly, 80 pages of A4. A similar 8″ disk will store roughly 132 pages of A4. The storage capacity of disks is increasing all the time, as is disk reliability.

A distributor will always tell you the sort of disks you can use on your system, and will usually recommend the make of disks to use. If you read a good catalogue of computer accessories, the types of disk available are described in detail, and the catalogue will probably tell you which disks you may use on your system. It is unwise to use inferior, cheap disks on a good system – your disks are likely to get corrupted and your work will be lost. Fig. 3.10 is an illustration of a floppy disk with its main features marked.

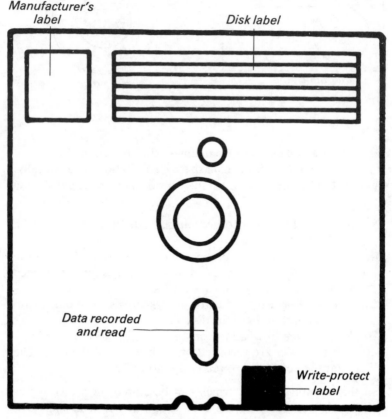

**Fig. 3.10**   A floppy disk

The round plastic disk inside its square protective covering is divided into tracks going round the disk and sectors going across it, not one continuous groove as on a gramophone record. Each track and sector is numbered and as data is stored, it is indexed with its track and sector number. When you want to call up or access a particular piece of work, the system refers to the index and very rapidly directs the reading heads to the correct part of the disk.

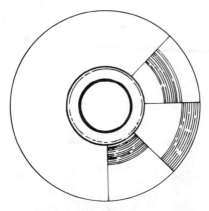

**Fig. 3.11**   How data is recorded on the disk

Sometimes small gaps are left when data is deleted from the disk, and if the Reclaim Disk Space facility (see Chapter 7) is used, then the data is sorted and re-indexed so that a small amount of disk space is made free to use again.

It is very important to take great care of your floppy disks:

**DO**
   −Store them carefully, away from magnetic fields.
   −Keep them in their protective envelopes when not in use.
   −Label them carefully.
   −Insert them carefully into the disk drive − without forcing or bending them.

**DON'T**
   −Put finger marks on the elongated slot where data is recorded and read.
   −Write on the label in ballpoint pen once the label is on the disk.

–Use pencil to write labels – the graphite might corrupt the disk.
–Leave disks lying around where they could be mishandled or
have things spilt on them.

**Winchester Disks**
Winchester Disks, which have to have a special disk drive, are really
small 'hard' disks. They are floppy disk size with a greater storage
capacity than floppy disks, but are rigid instead of being flexible.
Their storage capacity is not as great as that of a hard disk.

**Hard disks**
These work in exactly the same way as other disks, except that they
are rigid, are made of different material and have a far greater

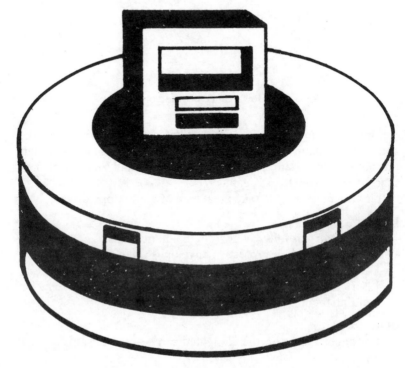

**Fig. 3.12** A hard disk

storage capacity (6 million characters). They too have special disk drives. They are protected by a special rigid plastic casing. Fig. 3.12 shows you what the casing of a hard, or cartridge, disk looks like.

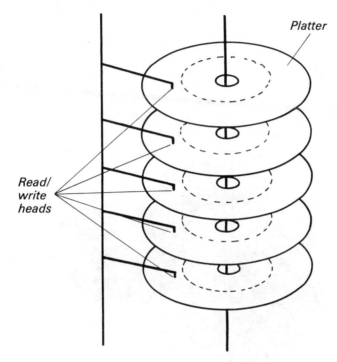

**Fig. 3.13** A hard disk pack

You can increase the storage capacity still further by having a pack of hard disks divided into platters with several read/write heads, as shown in Fig. 3.13.

The choice of which storage medium to use will depend on the amount of work to be stored, the size of the system you need and how much you can afford to pay. Hard disks are more expensive than floppy disks, but their greater storage capacity and consequent need to change disks less often might be more economical. Medium-sized and large systems tend to use hard disks, and small systems the floppy disks.

## Accessories

There are many accessories which can be bought to ease the path of word processing. Some are essential, some of great assistance and some would be considered necessary by some people and not by others. They can be divided into three main categories: printer accessories, disk storage accessories and general accessories.

### 1 Printer accessories

**Printwheels**   Printers will not work without a print head (or font) of some sort, which is therefore essential.

Daisy wheels are the most common form of print head, but thimbles are sometimes used (see Fig. 3.14).

**Fig. 3.14**   Common printwheels

Daisy wheels come in metal or plastic in a variety of type styles, and you have to make sure that the wheel is compatible with your printer. Some printers, too, will only take metal *or* plastic wheels rather than metal *and* plastic wheels. Metal printwheels last longer than plastic ones and give a sharper image. They are more expensive so you need to decide whether to use only a small number of different printwheels (which could be metal) or a large number (in which case you might prefer plastic).

The type styles available for your printer are usually set out on a large chart. You will need to choose the style or styles you want, and make sure that the wheel has on it the characters you want, check for the £ sign, fractions, percentage signs, vertical lines, accents, etc.

Fig. 3.15 shows some different type styles and pitches. You will notice how much less room a 15 pitch takes than a 10 pitch. It is advisable to have a backup printwheel for each different one you use, particularly if they are plastic – wheels do get broken or bent and they immediately become useless.

Binders or wallets in which to store your printwheels are sold so that they may be safely stored and quickly found.

---

This is an example of Cubic PS - Proportional Spacing

One of the most important things about word processing is the appearance of the finished product. Different typestyles and pitches can be used in the same document to emphasise a point or highlight a particular section.

This is an example of French Prestige Cubic - 12 pitch

One of the most important things about word processing is the appearance of the finished product. Different typestyles and pitches can be used in the same document to emphasise a point or highlight a particular section.

This is an example of Courier 10 UK - 10 pitch

One of the most important things about word processing is the appearance of the finished product. Different typestyles and pitches can be used in the same document to emphasise a point or highlight a particular section.

This is an example of Bilingual Gothic 15 - 15 pitch

One of the most important things about word processing is the appearance of the finished product. Different typestyles and pitches can be used in the same document to emphasise a point or highlight a particular section.

THIS IS AN EXAMPLE OF EMPHASIS 10 - 10 PITCH LOWER CASE

ONE OF THE MOST IMPORTANT THINGS ABOUT WORD PROCESSING IS THE APPEARANCE OF THE FINISHED PRODUCT. DIFFERENT TYPESTYLES AND PITCHES CAN BE USED IN THE SAME DOCUMENT TO EMPHASISE A POINT OR HIGHLIGHT A PARTICULAR SECTION.

---

**Fig. 3.15** Type or font styles and pitches (reduced size)

**Ribbons**   Another essential. Ribbons can be carbon (use once only) or fabric (use until too faint) and are usually housed in a cartridge (see Fig. 3.16).

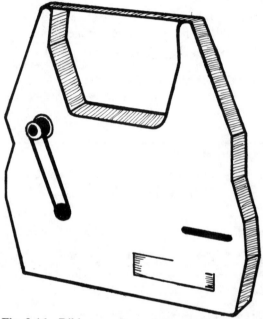

**Fig. 3.16**   Ribbon used on a daisy wheel printer

Again you will need to know the make and size of your printer when ordering ribbons. They can be bought singly but are more usually supplied in boxes of six or more.

There are also coloured ribbons – orange, yellow, blue, pink or brown, for example – but these are not available for every printer.

**Tractor feeders and single sheet feeders**   These are mechanisms which you attach to the printer for feeding through paper during a long print run.

*Tractor feeders* are used for continuous stationery. The stationery has holes at each side which fit into the sprockets on the feeder so that the stationery is fed through at an even pace. The feeders can cope with stationery as narrow as a strip of labels or as wide as the printer (normally A3 landscape). See Fig. 3.17.

**Fig. 3.17** A tractor or continuous stationery feeder

*Single sheet feeders* allow you to feed into the printer single sheets one at a time (see Fig. 3.18). Sometimes they have paper trays to house the paper, and sometimes hoppers.

Feeders are a comparatively costly accessory and are often fiddly to set up correctly. They are most useful for long print runs,

**Fig. 3.18** A single sheet feeder

although you need to check occasionally to make sure the paper has not jammed or come off its sprockets.

**Acoustic hoods**   Daisy wheel printers are noisy. It is worth considering having some sort of acoustic hood if there are several people (and printers) working in the same room. A hood can be a simple piece of plastic attached to the top of the printer at the front which partly cuts down the noise of the printing operation. It can also be an all-encasing plastic box which, when shut, almost completely shuts out the printing noise (see Fig. 3.19).

**Printout catchers and trolleys**   One of the problems of word processing is the amount of paper which has to be handled. If you are using continuous stationery a great deal, then it might be helpful, if you have the space, to invest in a trolley from which the paper can be fed into the printer, and which catches the paper and folds it as it emerges. Alternatively, there are free-standing *catchers* which can catch and fold the paper (see Fig. 3.20).

There are also, at the upper end of the market, printer stands on which to mount the printer, with paper feed racks and catching baskets incorporated (see Fig. 3.21).

## 2   Disk storage accessories
These range from simple folders for floppy disks to sturdy metal racks for storing large numbers of hard disks or disk packs.

The care of disks *is* very important, and so is the requirement for finding the right disk quickly, so that adequate disk storage facilities are very helpful. At first the number of disks you use is likely to be quite small, but it is surprising how quickly the number grows.

Fig. 3.22*a* shows a plastic desk top storage case for floppy disks, Fig. 3.22*b* a plastic floppy disk binder with envelopes and Fig. 3.22*c* a rack for storing hard disks. They all have easy identification facilities.

Disks in transit can cause problems, whether they are being sent through the post, taken on the underground where there are many electrical fields, or taken through the security checks at the airport. There are several containers which cater for these eventualities, and keep your disks safe from corruption. If you have a lot of work to send or take around the country or around the world, they are worth considering.

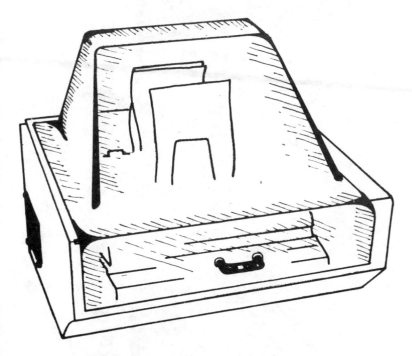

**Fig. 3.19**  An acoustic hood

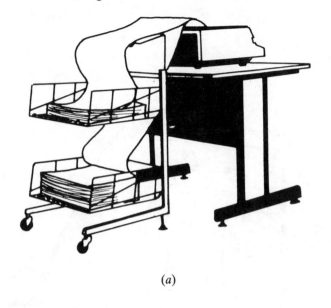

(*a*)

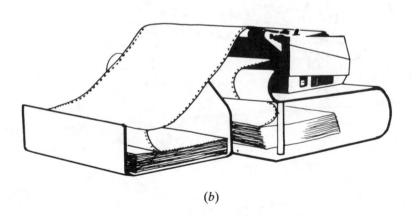

(*b*)

**Fig. 3.20**  Paper feeding and catching devices

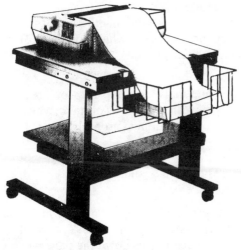

**Fig. 3.21** A printer stand, incorporating paper feeding and catching devices

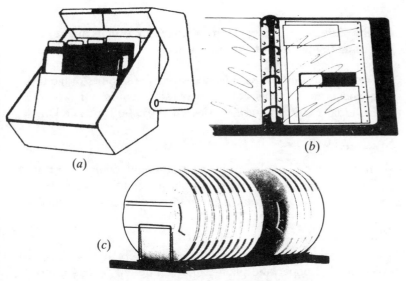

**Fig. 3.22** Disk storage accessories

**3   General accessories**
Some of these are more useful than others, and the best thing to do is to study the catalogues to see which you need. Here are some of them listed in alphabetical order, to give you some idea of what is available.

**Anti-static spray and mats**   Word processors, together with nylon clothing and carpets, can create a lot of static, which can prevent the word processor from functioning properly.

**Carrying cases**   Available for disks, tapes, personal computers.

**Cleaning kits**   These are available for screens, disk drive heads, hard disks, printers, etc.

**Copyholders**   These hold the paper from which you are copying work and can be free-standing on the desk or attached to the VDU with a line finder which moves down the page when you press the foot pedal.

**Footrests, tilt plinths and wrist supports**   Tilt plinths are for putting your VDU on when it has no height or tilt adjustment. Footrests perform a similar function for your feet, and wrist supports for your wrists.

**Rulers**   Special WP rulers help you to set up formats on the screen according to the pitch of your printwheel.

The only absolutely *essential* accessories are your storage disks, printwheels and ribbons. It is probably sufficient to start with these and gradually buy other accessories when you find you need them.

## Stationery

Word processing people rarely use 'traditional' computer printout stationery, because they need normal paper for reports, letters, specifications, etc. Normal paper and envelopes can, indeed, be used.

**1   Cut sheet paper**
If you are going to print out each sheet separately, then your normal office headed paper and plain paper can be fed by hand into the printer. It can also be fed in through a single sheet feeder.

If you are going to do long print runs on continuous stationery, then not only is a tractor feed very useful, but you will also need the special continuous stationery.

## 2 Continuous stationery

This comes in two main types:

(*a*) With guide holes in a strip down each side of the paper. The strip is removed when the paper has been through the printer, but unless it is of good quality, this can leave a rough edge (see Fig. 3.23*a*).

(*b*) Lightly glued to paper which itself has guide holes to attach to the tractor feed. The guide paper does not have to be A4 size and is removed from the fair copy paper by a gentle tug.

The paper can be plain or printed with the company's heading. Matching continuous stationery envelopes are also available. Forms, invoices, etc., can be printed on continuous stationery and no carbon required (NCR) paper can be supplied – printed if required.

Printers can normally take up to a thin card or two sheets of paper plus a carbon. Like typewriters, the platten can slip with constant use and sometimes envelopes will not 'turn up' properly.

## 3 Labels

Labels have become an essential part of the word processing scene. They are invaluable for large mail shots, when to put thousands of envelopes through the printer would become extremely tedious.

The labels are usually self-adhesive and either in continuous strips with the guide holes as for other types of continuous stationery (see Fig. 3.24*a*), or on sheets of A4 two, three or four labels wide, depending on the size (see Fig. 3.24*b*).

An economic and quicker way of providing labels, if the mailing list is one which is constantly in use, is to print the labels out on A4 sheets and then photocopy onto further sheets of labels as required.

Positioning paper in the printer can be a tricky operation, and sheets of paper are sometimes wasted while print adjustments are made. However, it is worth persevering with the correct stationery

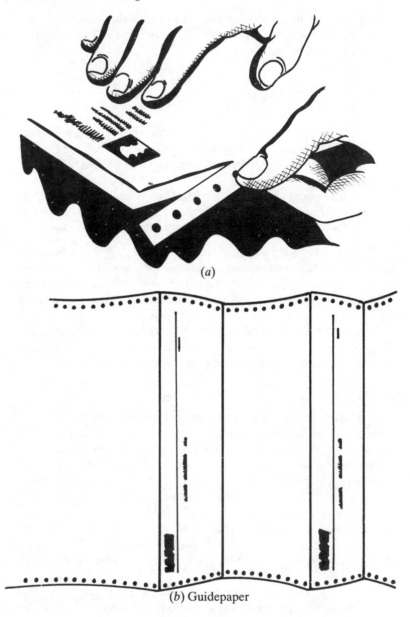

(*a*)

(*b*) Guidepaper

**Fig. 3.23**   Continuous stationery paper

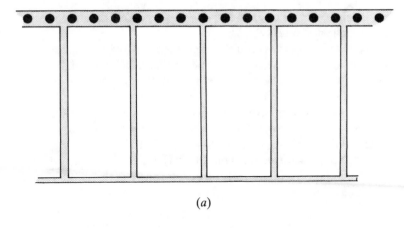

(a)

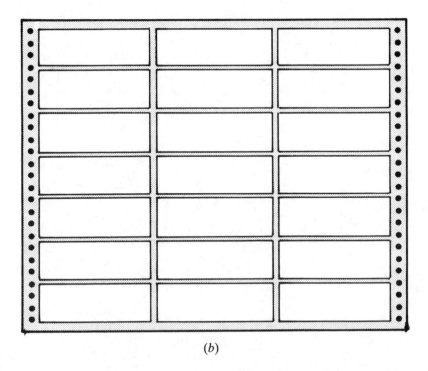

(b)

**Fig. 3.24** Continuous stationery labels

for a speedy and, above all, attractive printout, so that the finished product is of top quality.

This chapter has covered the ingredients needed to make word processing work: the hardware, the software, the essential access-ories and the stationery. Of these probably the most important is the software – wheels, ribbons and stationery can easily be changed, software cannot. It is better, in many instances, to find the software that *you* need for *your* work and then match it to the hardware on which it will run rather than to choose the hardware and then make do with the software which is not entirely what you want. A quality WP job is then completed with a good printer and stationery that will make your work look first-class.

# 4

# The Word Processing Environment

The main criterion for the environment in which word processing takes place is comfort for efficiency – if the environment is comfortable to work in, efficiency is likely to be greater. It is worth taking a little time and trouble to get the environment and the ergonomics right.

This chapter is not a series of recommendations based on thorough research, but rather a set of guidelines on topics which should be considered. Research has been done, and continues to be done, on various aspects of the use of VDUs, for example, and there are specialist publications available for those who want to study such subjects in depth.

## Furniture

A workstation is made up of:

–desk tops for terminals, printers and disk drives,
–the operator's chair,
–paper feeding and catching facilities,
–the WP hardware itself,
–adjuncts such as footrests and copyholders.

### 1  Desk tops

A word processing system needs more space than a typewriter does, and this must be thought about when the workstation is being prepared. The various pieces of hardware take up a lot of space in themselves, particularly a printer with a full acoustic hood. You have to remember, too, that space must be left for feeding in and catching continuous stationery, even if you have no devices for these functions.

Space is also needed on the desk top for such items as a lamp, a copyholder, a disk storage container (for floppy disks), an audio machine and handwritten or typed documents.

Some operators like to have the work from which they are copying on their left and some on their right, so space should be left on both sides of the keyboard. Stationery must be readily to hand and so must the printer if there is one printer per workstation. You also need room to be able to turn the platten control wheel on the side of the printer.

As well as sufficient space, the height of the working top is important. In some purpose-built workstations there is a facility for the keyboard and the screen to be at totally different heights and angles to suit the operator, and a special position for the printer. An operator would not wish to have to stand up every time a single page is printed out, so the printer must be at a convenient height for a seated operator. Fig. 4.1 shows a purpose-built workstation. If you are considering buying a purpose-built workstation, you should check that there is enough room for papers and disks on the desk top.

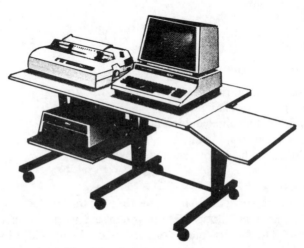

**Fig. 4.1**   A typical workstation

**2   Chairs**

A comfortable chair is an essential for anyone working at a word processor. The chair should be adjustable for height, so that the operator can sit with feet firmly on the ground, and with a good back support which is also adjustable for height and angle. The chair should also swivel and be mobile. In fact, a good typist's chair is quite suitable for word processing.

**3   Storage facilities**

You will need good storage facilities for stationery, print wheels, ribbons, manuals and, above all, disks. Ordinary metal filing cabinets and cupboards can be perfectly adequate, but they must be easily accessible.

Purpose-built furniture can certainly be comfortable and efficient to use. It is possible to put together a perfectly suitable workstation with the furniture which already exists, provided that the comfort and ergonomics are carefully taken into account.

## Lighting

Good lighting is extremely important, as in all work situations. The lighting should be sufficient to illuminate the surfaces from which work is being copied, whether flat on the desk or on a copy holder. At the same time lighting should not be directed straight onto the screen, which will cause glare and make the screen work difficult to read.

The ambient lighting should not be too harsh, but at the same time bright enough to let the operator work in comfort. Fixed strip lighting is acceptable, provided it is not too bright, and does not cause a reflection on the screen.

Ordinary daylight is naturally good to work in, provided that extra directional lighting is available for dull days, and blinds for very sunny days.

The best combination seems to be good daylight and ambient lighting for working after dark, plus directional lamps for working surfaces and copyholders, as required. Lighting which is too harsh or bright can tire the eyes; lighting which is too dim can strain them.

## Atmosphere

### 1   Temperature

Fortunately, word processors are able to work in normal office or home conditions, and do not need the closely-controlled atmosphere of a large mainframe computer. However, they are susceptible to certain atmospheric conditions.

If the room temperature is very much too hot or too cold, then not only will the operator find it difficult to work, so will the machine. A CPU set near the window on a very hot, sunny day has been known to blow a fuse. A comfortable working temperature is what is required, without extremes of hot and cold.

### 2   Static

As mentioned in the previous chapter, static can build up in the atmosphere, particularly where a lot of man-made fibre is used. This may result in the operator getting small shocks off the equipment, or the equipment itself malfunctioning. Anti-static mats to put under the hardware or to stand on are available, as are anti-static sprays for carpets.

### 3   Pollution and power

Word processors are affected by pollution. Smoke, especially, can damage the read/write heads in the disk drive – it is wise not to smoke when working with a word processor. Spilt liquids and crumbs can also be damaging to the equipment, so that an area should be set aside for coffee and biscuits rather than allowing these to be consumed at the workstation. No smoking, eating or drinking is a sensible rule for word processing.

Dust can also cause problems. If you watch the engineer clean out the disk drives, particularly the air filter, you will be impressed by the amount of dust which can collect. An efficient vacuum cleaner is better than a carpet sweeper for cleaning the carpet, so that dust is not swirled around the room. It is advisable, as far as possible, to prevent dust and dirt from entering the room from outside.

A word processor needs a regular, stable supply of power. On larger systems it might be advisable to ensure that it is always plugged in to a 'clean' line – that is, a power source that is specially installed for the system alone. Vacuum cleaners, audio machines and other electrical devices should not be plugged in to a 'clean' line. A power source used only for the system will guard against sudden surges and diminutions in the power supply which can affect the system and cause the loss of a considerable amount of data.

A word processing system will work perfectly well in a normal, comfortable, healthy atmosphere – care should be taken to guard against extremes.

## Décor

A pleasing décor can help to make the working conditions more comfortable. WP operators look up (at the screen for screen messages and proof-reading) more than a copy typist would, and for this reason the wall, or other objects at which an operator looks, is significant.

If working towards a wall, the operator should be able to look at something unobtrusive and restful: bright and patterned surfaces are unhelpful. It can be tiring for the operator to be looking directly at a clear window. Very often workstations are set in clusters, at different angles, so that when the operator looks up there is no one directly opposite, and the whole set-up is conducive to concentration.

Screens should be positioned so that direct sunlight, daylight or artificial light does not cause glare and difficulty in reading what is on the screen. If glare is a real problem, then a specially-coated 'filter', which can be fixed onto the screen to help reduce glare and at the same time maintain the clarity of the VDU image, is available.

Even with very basic lighting, heating, furniture and other facilities, the working environment and atmosphere can be comfortable, if a little foresight and common sense are used. Much will depend on the use that is made of what is available.

## People

People come in all shapes and sizes, and should be prepared to adjust heights, angles, lighting, heating, ventilation and brightness to suit themselves and any others with whom they work.

People say they get backache from doing word processing for long periods at a time, or feel strained across the back or shoulders. This is probably true if the chair and desk height is wrong, if the seating is not adjustable and if the operator uses a slovenly posture. In a normal, healthy person backache should not occur if all the ergonomics are right, the person uses all the facilities correctly and sits up straight.

Again, people say they get eye-strain from using a VDU for long periods. This may well be so, but it is worth examining the possible causes of the eyestrain. It might be the lighting; it might be the positioning of the screen opposite a window or with strong light falling directly onto it; it might be the brightness or flicker rate of the screen – the former can certainly be controlled. It might also well be that the operator is wearing spectacles that are incorrect for the work in hand, or not wearing spectacles when they are required. Operators who wear bi-focals find it particularly tiring to keep looking down at paper and then up onto a screen. Anyone who is in any doubt about their eyesight and any eyestrain from which they may suffer, should consult an optician who knows about the hazards of intensive VDU work. Many firms offer this facility free to their operators as part of their working conditions.

Long periods of work at a VDU can be very exhausting, as can many other forms of intensive work. Great concentration is needed for accurate WP work. Periods of rest, or periods of doing something else (taking a coffee break or delivering work, for example) can be very beneficial. A variety of work also helps overcome the tiredness sometimes engendered by intense concentration. Most people cannot be expected to work at a VDU for several hours non-stop. If they do this, then comfort, efficiency and productivity will decrease.

Two aspects of working with VDUs do cause concern – pregnancy and epilepsy. It is not within the scope of this book to examine these two conditions, but if concern *is* felt by women likely to become pregnant or by people who suffer from epilepsy, then they should take advice from someone knowledgeable in the field.

## Tidy working

Most of what has been said in this chapter is common sense, and applies to working conditions generally. Tidy working is also common sense.

**Fig. 4.2**

An untidy working environment will almost certainly cause less efficiency, and could be dangerous. A word processor is a safe piece of machinery with which to work if normal safety precautions are taken. Trailing cables are a definite hazard. Avoid putting your fingers in the printer while it is printing out. Turn it off when changing wheels and ribbons. Do not let ties or jewellery dangle in the printer if you are standing over it. Excessive hand jewellery and long finger nails can make your keying less accurate. Try not to use electric bar fires to keep your feet warm in winter; fan heaters or convector heaters are much safer. If you are using a full acoustic hood make sure you open it fully when you are using the printer, so that the edge of the hood is *not* on a level with your eyes.

In fact, working tidily and safely is the most comfortable, and therefore efficient, way to work. Fig. 4.2 illustrates what is meant!

# 5

# How to Start Word Processing

The time eventually arrives when you have prepared and read as much as you are able, and you have to take the plunge and start working on the machine itself. This is, perhaps, a time of trepidation if you have never set hands on an electronic keyboard before, but one precept to bear very firmly in mind is *don't worry*. There is usually very little you can do that will harm the machine in any way. You may well get it wrong, or get yourself in a muddle which will take time and patience to untangle, but irretrievable damage to your system is very rare.

This chapter will take you through the steps of getting your machine ready, using it and closing it down. If you attend training sessions on a particular machine, you will often find that you start learning at the 'using' part of the sequence – getting the machine ready has been done for you. However, it is assumed here that you are teaching yourself and that no assistance, other than an instruction manual, is available.

Of course, when you are learning to use a particular machine you will need to follow the instruction manual supplied with it – just as you would for using a power drill or a washing machine. The instruction manual may well use not only words with which you are unfamiliar, but turns of phrase which have developed from the technical terms used in computers and which can seem difficult – or even incomprehensible – on first reading. Again, don't worry, follow the instructions carefully and logically and you will succeed in making your machine work.

Again, different sizes and types of system (whether shared logic or stand alone, for example) will require different ways of making the machine work, but in the end every system follows much the same pattern, and once you have established the principles of how to make one system work, those principles are fairly easily transferred to other systems.

## Getting started

Assume, then, that your hardware has been assembled and that you have a disk with your word processing software on it. You also have a blank disk on which you intend to store the work you wish to do. The first of these disks is often called your *system disk* or your *software disk*, and the second your *work disk* or your *storage disk*.

### 1   Switch on
It may seem an obvious thing to say, but do not forget to switch the system on – all parts of it. Very often the screen, the disk drive and the printer all have separate on/off switches. On some systems it is necessary to switch on the various parts in a given sequence, so follow the instructions carefully.

### 2   Load the software/log on
**Small systems**   Your system disk will have to be inserted in your disk drive. If you are working on floppy disks, this will mean literally taking the disk out of its protective envelope and putting it in the correct slot in the disk drive. It is always important to get the disk the right way up and the right way round and in the correct drive, so again follow the instructions carefully. Usually you will then have to press a specific key or keys to get the system up and running and after a short wait the first *menu* or instructions will appear on the screen. A menu is simply a list of options from which you may choose – exactly like a restaurant menu. Getting the system up and running is called *booting* it – pulling it up by its bootstraps! If the system goes down, or fails, then you will have to re-boot it. If you are working on hard disks, then the system disk will already be in the disk drive and the very act of switching on will normally produce the first menu or instructions on the screen. On the larger floppy disks, the software disk and work disk can be one and the same, so that only the one disk will need to be inserted.

**Large systems**   If the screen on which you are working is a terminal attached to a large, mainframe computer, then you will have no disk to insert, but after switching on, the first instructions or menu to appear on the screen will probably ask you to key in a password to connect your terminal in to the main computer. This is often called *logging on*, and you may well be invited to LOGON?. Your work will also be stored on the large disks, so you will have no need to 'initialize' a disk as you would have to do on a small system.

### 3   Initialize your work disk (floppy)
The blank floppy disk you intend as your Work Disk must be *initialized* before you can store any work on it. This is sometimes called *formatting* your disk.

Usually the first menu or instructions to appear on the screen will include the option of INITIALIZE or FORMAT disk. This is the option you will need to use for initializing your first work disk. To initialize a disk means to prepare it for working with a particular machine – to make it compatible with the machine and able to understand the instructions written into the software.

You will need to put your blank disk into the appropriate disk drive and follow through the instructions given on the screen and/or in the manual to initialize the disk and prepare it for work.

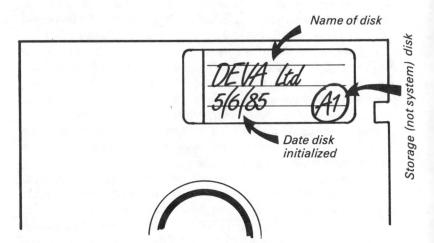

**Fig. 5.1**   A disk label

Once the initializing or formatting process is completed, then the *essential* step to take is to *label* your disk. The information generally needed on a label is the date, whether it is a work disk or a system disk, and the general nature of the work most likely to be stored on that disk. A typical disk label is shown in Fig. 5.1.

When labelling your disk:

**Do** write the label *before* you put it on the disk.

**Do not** use pencil. The graphite in the lead can 'corrupt' the disk a little.

The general care of disks was described more fully in Chapter 3.

Your system disk and work disk are both now ready and you need to 'get into' the word processing software to start work.

### 4  Load the word processing program

If you have initialized your work disk, then normally the system will automatically have returned to the main menu or instructions. If no disk initialization was necessary, then the first menu or instructions will be on the screen anyway.

The screen and/or the manual will tell you how to *load* the WP program from the system disk onto your screen. Usually pressing one or two specific keys is all that is required and sometimes a message saying LOADING will appear on the screen. Again a short wait will give the machine time to load the software instructions from the system disk into the terminal on which you will be working.

### 5  Key in the date and/or time and other figures

On some large systems you are required to key in the date and/or the time before the program can be loaded. If this is the case then you must key in the date, etc., *exactly* as instructed.

For example, for 2 June 1986 if the instruction reads: KEY IN DATE DD/MM/YY, then you must key in 02/06/86, not forgetting the oblique strokes. If you key in 02.06.86, then it is likely that the machine will not recognise that you mean 02/06/86 and will indicate that you have made an error.

Notice, too, that for dates and times – and for much other figure work on computers – if the figure is a single one, then it is important to key in the zero as well, so that 02 cannot in any way be confused with 20. Indeed the computer probably will not recognise that '2' on its own means '02' and will indicate that you have made an error.

Another very important point to remember is that when keying in figures you *must* use the zero and not a capital letter 'O', as one tends to do in typewriting. A zero on a computer screen will often appear as 0̸. Sometimes it will appear as an 0̸ on the printout and sometimes as a normal nought (0). Equally a small letter 'l' is not acceptable as the figure one. The key labelled 1 *must* be used.

So, for example, if the instructions are:

KEY IN TIME HH/MM/SS

then for half past one in the afternoon you must key in

13/30̸/0̸0̸

The 24 hour clock is normally used. Remember to use the figure one and the zero as required.

Finally, when keying in numerals with other symbols such as the oblique or a stop, remember to key in *exactly* as you are instructed, and do not leave spaces unless told to do so. The computer is likely to recognise:

12/12/86

for 12 December 1986, but would not recognise:

12 / 12 / 86

It would also not recognise an extra space keyed in inadvertently:

12 /12/86

So if, when keying in dates, times, names that you are perhaps asking the computer to compare with data already stored in its memory – to recognise, in fact – then make sure that what you are keying in is absolutely accurate. Stops, spaces, zeros, ones and other symbols matter – use them accurately.

## Screen messages

One of the most useful things to do when learning word processing is to read and interpret screen messages. A learner, not being used to reading messages as a result of an instruction given, will tend to ignore them, but screen messages are there to help and should be attended to.

There are several types of screen messages, which can be roughly categorised as:

1   Information,
2   Instructions,
3   Error messages.

### 1   Information
There is normally, when keying in or editing is taking place, a certain amount of information on the screen, sometimes on one line at the top or bottom of the screen, called the *status line*. Sometimes more information on the 'status' of the text is given than can be contained on one line; then, obviously, more than one line is taken up, which can intrude on the text on the screen, so that the system will allow you to dispense with the information when it is not required.

The sort of information given about the 'status' of a document is:

–the number of the line on which you are working;
–the number of the character or column across the page you have reached;
–the number of the page on which you are working;
–whether you are 'writing' the document on which you are working or whether you are merely 'reading' it;
–when a function is in progress, and you have to wait for the computer to finish – 'operation in progress' is a common message;
–'please wait' is another common message.

As is the case throughout, different systems will give different information in different ways, but it is important to read and take note of them as soon as possible.

### 2   Instructions
(*a*)   Instructions often come in the form of options. The message will, perhaps, say:

SELECT FUNCTION

and give a list of alternative functions, of which the operator must choose one.

A typical list of options might be:

I   for insert
D   for delete
A   for add

The operator would then key in I, or D, or A as required, and usually press the ENTER or RETURN or ACTION or similar key to confirm the instruction given.

(*b*)   Another common method of asking the operator to give the required commands is to tell the operator which key(s) to press to take the process on to the next step. Typically the message would be:

PRESS ENTER TO CONTINUE, CANCEL TO ABORT

This means you must press ENTER if you want to say 'Yes, please – this is what I want to do', or CANCEL if you want to say 'No, I don't want to do that.'

The message is often simplified to 'Y' for 'Yes, please continue', and 'N' for 'No thank you, stop' – it depends on the way the software was written. The word *abort*, which seems somewhat emotive to those unfamiliar with computer jargon, normally just means to stop.

(*c*)   A third common way of giving instructions to the operator is in fact to ask what the operator wants to do next. Instead of saying SELECT FUNCTION or GIVE COMMAND, the message FUNCTION? or COMMAND? will appear on the screen. Sometimes the question mark flashes to draw attention to the fact that a command is required. In this case there are often several commands which *could* be given: too many to list on the screen at the time, but which will be detailed in the instruction manual.

(*d*)   The fourth way of giving screen messages in this category is to set out a series of instructions and ask the operator to confirm that they are right or to amend as necessary.

For example, when printing out documents there are various print commands to be given, and a menu to indicate the requirements of the work to be printed might be laid out as follows:

TOP MARGIN $\boxed{01}$ BOTTOM MARGIN $\boxed{09}$
PITCH (10, 12, 15, P) $\boxed{10}$ SPACING 1, 1.5, 2, 2.5, 3 $\boxed{1.0}$
JUSTIFICATION (Y, N) $\boxed{N}$ CONTINUOUS UNDER-
LINING (Y, N) $\boxed{Y}$

The operator could alter the figures or letters in the boxes as required. For example, if double spacing instead of single was needed, then 1.0 would be altered to 2.0 When all is correct, the message at the bottom of this very simple print menu might read:

PRESS ENTER TO CONFIRM *or* KEY Y TO CONFIRM

So, in one WP software program, the operator will very likely come across several different ways of receiving instructions from the computer and giving instructions to it.

## 3 Error messages

Error messages range from the simple and helpful to the obscure and terrifying.

The message INCORRECT DATE, PLEASE TRY AGAIN would very soon tell you that you have made a mistake in keying in the date, as illustrated earlier in the chapter. For exactly the same mistake, the message could read SYNTAX ERROR, which to a beginner would mean little or nothing. Generally speaking, word processing software is becoming more 'user friendly' and helpful. Self-explanatory messages such as:

DOCUMENT ALREADY EXISTS when you are trying to
name a new document,
*or* DOCUMENT NOT FOUND when you are trying to locate a
document,
*or* DISK FULL,
*or* RIBBON OUT to tell you why the printer has stopped,

are the ones most commonly used. Messages which indicate a small mistake on the part of the operator – a keying in error or an incorrect command given – are sometimes accompanied by a short, audible 'bleep' to draw the operator's attention to the message.

There are, however, error messages which tell the operator about system malfunctions. These can be rather alarming, and must be read and acted upon. They can be a simple message such as:

DISK NOT READY

which means that you have forgotten to initialize the disk or it has not been put properly into the disk drive.

PRINTER NOT READY

probably means that you have forgotten to switch it on.

They can be rather more serious such as:

SYSTEM ERROR

which can mean that you have given the computer conflicting commands which it cannot understand or that there is a slight flaw in the system – perhaps the system disk is beginning to wear out. This sort of message means that you must stop and think about what you have done, try it again, and if the same message still appears, then the fault is rather serious and steps to remedy it should be taken. Most manuals will tell you what to do if this sort of message appears on the screen.

An even more serious message is:

DISK UNUSABLE
*or* FATAL SYSTEM ERROR

DISK UNUSABLE might just mean that a backup disk will put you back in business again, but FATAL SYSTEM ERROR usually means a call to the engineer. Again the manual will normally tell you what to do.

Screen messages are an extremely important part of word processing. At first the tendency is to ignore them, or even simply not to see them. Once having learnt to read and interpret them, however, another danger can be that the operator expects a message to appear for every little thing which goes wrong. Screen messages are there to help – and they can be a great help if intelligently used.

## Command and edit

We will assume that now the machine is switched on, the disks are ready and correctly inserted and that the software program is loaded, ready to begin word processing. There will be a message of some sort on the screen inviting you to select a function or give a command.

One of the first principles of word processing, as with any computer, is that the word processor needs to be told what to do. The WP is not a thought reader – it is but a machine and will only do exactly what it is told, no more and no less. What is more, it will only do *precisely* what it is told, and it is always right – much to the frustration of many an operator who can often be heard to say 'No, no, I didn't mean that' while the machine is carrying out exactly the instructions it has been given. It follows, therefore, that there must be some way of telling the machine what to do, and these instructions are generally known as *commands*.

Another fundamental principle of word processing, as has already been described, is that it is very easy to make corrections and manoeuvres of various sorts to text already keyed in, and this is known as *editing*.

Sometimes commands have to be given *before* editing can take place, sometimes commands need to be given *while* editing is taking place, and sometimes commands must be given *after* editing has taken place; it very much depends upon the way in which the software has been written and the nature of the command required. The instruction manual which accompanies the system will tell you (not always very clearly, it must be admitted) in which order things must be done.

There is one thing which is well-nigh universal and applies to virtually all systems – when in *command mode* (giving commands) whatever you key in will come out in capital letters on the screen, whether you have used the SHIFT key (for upper case letters and symbols) or not. In *edit mode* the characters will come out on the screen, and on the printout, in small *or* capital letters as required.

You must, therefore, be able to make the distinction between being in command mode and edit mode, and to know in your own mind whether you are aiming to give commands or to key in and manipulate text – to edit.

On some systems your very first page of work can be keyed in straight away onto a blank screen without any command being given at all. On many, you have to command the system to 'open a file' before you can start keying in. Again, the screen itself and the instruction manual will tell you what you must do first.

## Opening a file (creating a document)

At a very early stage in word processing – either before you begin keying anything in or just as soon as the first page has been keyed in and needs to be stored on your work disk – you will need to 'open a file' or 'create a document' on your work disk. Inevitably the way you do this, the commands you have to give and the order in which things must be done will vary from machine to machine, but there are some basic rules to bear in mind.

Opening a WP file is, in a sense, just like opening, or starting, a file of papers in an office. The file has to be given a name and a description and stored in the right place so that it can be quickly found according to the filing index. It then has to be opened before any pages can be put into it.

In the same way, a computer file has to be opened, named, described and stored away so that it can be quickly found again. A 'file' in word processing is often called a 'document', but the same principles apply.

### 1   Creating a file

First the WP must be told that you wish to open a file – it must be given the right command. On some systems this will mean calling up the appropriate menu; on some it will mean selecting a specific function from a general menu; on some it will mean pressing given function keys or designated QWERTY keys to give the desired command. There may be systems on which other means have been designed to create and open a file, but the three mentioned above are the most common.

### 2   Naming the document

On some systems the next file to be opened will automatically be allocated the next available number, but on most the operator will actually be required to give the document a name.

Each system will have its own rules about the combination of letters and figures (alphanumeric) which may be used and the limits within which the operator must work. Usually letters and figures *can* be combined and sometimes stops and other symbols may be used. Usually a space is read by the computer as the end of a name.

For example REPORT1 is usually an acceptable name;

REPORT.1 could well be accepted; REPORT 1 would be read by the WP as REPORT only or not accepted at all.

It is a great temptation when starting work on the WP to use one's own name or initials, or those of the originator of the work, to name the document (ANN or JWP for example). It is better, however, to try to give the document a name that has some meaning and will help to indicate the nature of the document to be created. Even REPORT is rather general and some indication of what the report is about (SALEREP – sales report – for example) will help to distinguish the document from others of a like nature which might be written. SALEREP could then be followed by a number indicating which sales report it is – SALEREP1, SALEREP2, etc. – provided that the naming capacity is great enough to take that number of alphanumeric characters.

Each office or section of an office will no doubt devise its own system for naming documents. The important thing then is to stick to the system.

### 3   Describing the document
Most systems allow you space, when naming a document, to give a brief description of the document. The description usually comes up on the index or catalogue, and can be extremely helpful in identifying a document when it is required after a lapse of time. The message here, then, is – do use the description facility, and use it intelligently.

The facility should allow you to enter a comprehensible abbreviated description of the document and, above all, the date – if this is not done automatically when you load the software or log on.

For example, our document SALEREP1 could well bear the description: 'SALES REPORT JAN TO JUNE 15/08/85' while SALEREP2 could be 'SALES REPORT JUL TO DEC 16/01/86'. There would be no doubt about the contents of the document when looking it up in the future.

It might be wise when opening a file which you know is going to be stored for some time to maintain a hard copy catalogue or index of all documents and the disks where they are to be found. The rationale for doing this and various methods of recording the information are discussed more fully in Chapter 7, but it should be noted here that the *time* to put document details into a manually maintained catalogue is when the file is first opened/the document is first created on the word processor.

Once a file has been opened, then 'pages' can be added to it at will. The way in which this is done varies, naturally, but there are two main ways in which documents can be keyed in and subsequently stored on disk. These are the page-based and the document-based systems.

## Document-based and page-based systems

You will find that, generally speaking, your system is either page-based or document-based. Each has its advantages and disadvantages and will dictate a different way of working on long documents. The first text on which you work is unlikely to be more than one page long, unless you are using a screen-based training programme, but it is advisable that at an early stage you should establish whether you are working on a document- or a page-based system.

### 1   Document-based systems

On these systems you key in your work, taking, at the keying in stage, no particular notice of where the pages are to be broken (that is, how many lines there will be on the printed page). When the document is printed out it will automatically be broken into pages for you after a set number of lines per page. (You will always have an opportunity at the printing stage to override the page break instructions if you wish, and make your pages longer or shorter.) At the keying in stage, then, you just continue keying in your work until the whole document is complete. You will have followed the instructions on the screen or the menu to tell the system that you wish to 'write' a new document and what its name will be.

The main *advantages* of this system are:

1   There is no need to watch for the ends of pages at the keying in stage.
2   It is easy to move text around within the document when it comes to the editing stage.
3   If large pieces of extra text need to be inserted, this can very easily be done.

The main *disadvantages* are:

1   Unless care is taken pages will often be broken at an inappropriate place – in the middle of a paragraph or table, for example.
2   Page numbers and footnotes can appear at the top of the next page instead of at the bottom of the correct page (this is known as 'widows and orphans').
3   It can take an extremely long time for the system to find a particular page to edit and particularly to print out.

## 2   Page-based systems

On these systems you key in your work (and store it on the disk, if required) page by page – you must take note of the number of lines you want on the printed page and not go beyond this on the screen page (which is normally longer). *After* the page has been keyed in, you will 'write' it to your storage disk. Very often you can print out the work which is on the screen without storing it on the disk.

So, on a document of, say, ten pages, you would key in each page and 'write' it to your disk – with or without printing out each page as you go along. Most good systems will then allow you to print out the whole document, while doing other work on the screen, and to break the pages at different points if you should wish to do so.

This means, of course, that you will need to find out early in your learning how to get from page to page and how to find a specific page in a document already stored.

The main *advantages* of the page-based system are:

1   You can print out each page as you go along, which can be useful for proof-reading and rough copies.
2   You need not open a file, on some systems, if all you require is to print out what is on the screen and then lose it.
3   You have more instant control over the page endings– you are less likely to have widows and orphans.
4   It is fairly easy and quick to find a specific page in a long document and edit it or print it out.

The main *disadvantages* are:

1   It is not normally so easy to move text from page to page as it is on the document-based system.
2   You have to take notice of the length of each page and adjust

accordingly – particularly if you are going to print out in double (etc.) spacing.

3   It can be very complicated to insert large chunks of additional text, particularly if it means moving existing bits of text onto the next page, which in turn becomes too long and so on. This can be a serious disadvantage if very long documents with many additions to the first draft are frequently required.

So, get to know whether your system is document-based or page-based. At first you will find it does not matter which it is, but as you get more skilled and need to do more complicated things you will have to be careful to use your system – whichever it is – in the most efficient way.

One thing you should *not* do is confuse a system that is document- or page-based with a system that is menu- or code-based. Document- or page-based refers to the *structure* of the work keyed in; menu- or code-based refers to the *method of giving instructions* or commands.

## Menu- and code- or command-based systems

### 1   Menu-based systems
When a system is menu-based, as has been mentioned previously, it means that the user is presented with a series menu of options from which to choose. Fig. 5.2 gives an example of a simple menu for a *document-based* system.

> R = to read a document
> W = to write a document
> D = to delete a document
> E = to edit a document
> Key in required letter and press ENTER

**Fig. 5.2**

Fig. 5.3 gives an example of a menu for a *page-based* system.

> R = to read the current page
> N = to read the next page
> V = to read the previous page
> L = to read the last page
> Press R, N, V or L and then RETURN

**Fig. 5.3**

As you can see, a menu can be used for a document- or a page-based system. It is normally easier to operate, particularly in the initial stages of learning, than a code-based system. This is because the menus will offer you several options and instructions on the screen and you do not have to memorise lots of codes for your commands.

**2   Code- or command-based systems**

This is when the commands given to perform the various functions are not listed down on a menu and have to be remembered. Usually the codes are very obvious, such as RP for Read Page, PP for Print Page, DD for Delete Document, etc. Sometimes, the codes are rather more complicated and the user has to press a CONTROL key and a QWERTY key simultaneously before giving the required commands.

On a code-based system, instead of a menu the screen is normally blank except for an invitation (at the top or bottom of the screen) to give the required command, as already mentioned.

As you can imagine, it is not easy at first to remember all the codes for the commands, but if the system is used frequently, the codes become embedded in the user's memory and can be quickly keyed in. If the menu-based system is too lengthy – that is, if the user has to go through several menus to perform a fairly commonplace function – then once the user is thoroughly familiar with the system, it can be rather tedious. Many systems have a mixture of menus and coded commands but it is likely that each individual system will be predominantly menu-based or code-based.

Just as in page- or document-based systems, menu- or code-based systems each have their advantages and disadvantages – the perfect WP software has yet to be written.

## The three stages of WP

The process of word processing can be broken down into three distinct stages:

**Stage 1**   Getting the text right on the screen.
**Stage 2**   Storing the text on disk (or other storage medium).
**Stage 3**   Recalling and/or printing text.

Let us examine these three stages in detail.

**STAGE 1  Getting the text right on the screen**

**Keying in**  You may find that your screen has some status line messages or you may be faced with a completely blank screen – as ever, the systems vary. You may, indeed, find your screen filled with little dots to represent the number of characters it is possible to fit into the screen.

What every screen will have, however, is the *cursor*. The cursor will identify to the computer whereabouts on the screen you are operating, so you must know how to move the cursor left and right, up and down, and for this you will need to use the *cursor control keys*.

Sometimes these keys are ordinary QWERTY keys which have been given the additional function of moving the cursor about, but more normally the cursor control keys are to be found in a separate 'pad' of keys and are simply keys with arrows marked on them (see Fig. 5.4).

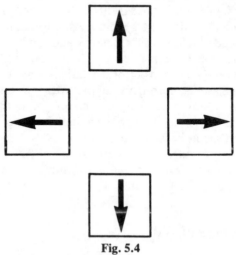

**Fig. 5.4**

Press the key marked $\rightarrow$ to move the cursor to the right, the key marked $\downarrow$ to move it down the screen and so on. One light press will move it one space in the required direction, but if you hold the key down then the 'repeat' effect comes into operation, and the cursor will move quickly up or down, to left or right. On some systems you might not be able to move the cursor with the control keys until you have keyed in some text.

When you first start using a WP the cursor seems to move very quickly, but after a while you find you want to move the cursor more rapidly still, and there are usually keys which, when pressed, will allow you to move the cursor from word to word, to the beginning or end of the line, straight to the top or bottom of the text, etc. Again the keys are sometimes normal QWERTY keys with a dual function, but more often than not they are *dedicated* keys with names that show their use quite clearly. A typical pad of cursor control keys is shown in Fig. 5.5.

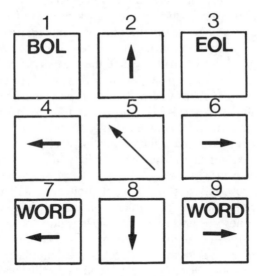

**Fig. 5.5**   A pad of cursor control keys

Key 1 moves cursor to Beginning of Line
Key 2 moves cursor up the screen, line by line
Key 3 moves cursor to End of Line
Key 4 moves cursor to the left, letter by letter
Key 5 moves cursor to top left-hand corner of screen
Key 6 moves cursor to the right, letter by letter
Key 7 moves cursor to the left, word by word
Key 8 moves cursor down the screen, line by line
Key 9 moves cursor to the right, word by word

Some machines allow you to pinpoint where on the screen you wish to work by use of a 'mouse', and others by touch screen. A *mouse* is a small spherical control mechanism which you roll to left or right, up or down, to move the cursor to the required position – there are no keys to press. The *touch screen* system allows you to identify in which part of the screen you wish to work by simply touching the screen itself. However, the most usual method of instructing the machine whereabouts on the screen you wish to work is by means of the cursor control keys, and these you will need to use a great deal of the time. Their use should be learnt early in any training programme.

When keying in text you will find that the cursor keeps pace with you and is at the last character you have keyed in.

Almost all word processors have the wraparound facility, which means that as you come to the end of a line the machine will automatically wrap the text round onto the next line for you. *You do not need to press the key* (often called the RETURN) which is equivalent to a carriage return on a typewriter. A word at the end of a line will not be broken in the middle – the whole word will be transferred automatically onto the next line. So you can just keep on keying in the text without having to make carriage returns. You will find the keyboard very light – much lighter than an electric typewriter – and that your text tends to run away with you, but don't worry, corrections are easy to make.

You may be wondering at this point about setting margins. Most systems have pre-set margins which you can alter at a later stage if the pre-set ones are unsuitable for a particular document. When margins are pre-set, then the system is said to *default* to those margins. The term is also used for pitch sizes, etc.: a system which 'defaults' to 10 pitch, for example, means that it will always print out in 10 pitch unless instructed otherwise. If you need to set margins *before* typing in the text, then your instructions should tell you what to do.

You *will* need to press the RETURN key (or its equivalent) at the end of a paragraph, and will probably need to press RETURN a second time to create a blank line between paragraphs.

Otherwise the QWERTY part of the keyboard is used very much as though it were a typewriter keyboard, including the SHIFT keys. You may find that these keys are set in very slightly different positions from standard typewriter shift keys, but the difference is minimal and you will quickly get used to it.

**Corrections** Keying-in errors can very easily be corrected. In Assignment 1 the underlined words show some common errors, which can be corrected as described below. There is no need to key in this assignment, but you should study it closely.

**Assignment 1**

```
                    WORD PROCESSING


        Word  processing  has  been  used  in  many
        large   copmanies   now   for   some   years,
        particularly  in  London  and  other  major
        cities.  However,  its  spread  into  medium-
        sized  and  small  firms  has  been  slower
        than predicted.

        the benefits of word processing are still
        not  apreciated  by  many businessmen; they
        do  not  seem  to  realise  that,  properly
        used,  it  can  increase  produtivity  and
        enhance    job    satisfaction,    fully
        joustifying   the   initial   capital
        investment.
```

*Mistake 1* is two characters reversed. In most systems, move the cursor to the 'p' and simply key in 'm' followed by 'p'.

*Mistake 2* is a required character which has been omitted. Move the cursor to where the insertion is required, press a key which allows you to insert the missing character (called INSERT, CHAR INSERT, BREAK or something similar), key in the required 'p' and re-align the text (close the gap up again).

*Mistake 3* is again a required character which has been omitted. The same action is required, starting with the cursor on the letter 't'.

*Mistake 4* is an unwanted character which must be deleted. Move the cursor to the 'o' and press the appropriate DELETE key or keys.

So, the principle for correcting keying errors is:

Pinpoint the mistake on the screen by using the cursor control keys,
Make the required correction.

**Keying in and correcting your work**    Assignment 2 will allow you to do some keying in of your own. You will note that it has no headings, but is simple, straightforward text. You may well make mistakes in your keying in, even if you are a proficient typist. The following general principles of text correction might help you correct your own errors:

1   Position the cursor where the correction is needed. Use the cursor control keys to move the cursor to the exact position on the screen where the mistake has occurred.
2   If the character is incorrect simply type in (overtype!) the correct one. Note that on some machines it is necessary to delete the incorrect character before keying in the correct one.
3   If a character is unwanted, delete it (look for a key marked DELETE or CHARACTER DELETE or something like that).
4   If a character is omitted, make room for the additional character by pressing the required key (often called INSERT, CHAR(acter) INSERT or BREAK), key in the required character and instruct the machine to close up the space again – to re-align the text.
5   Where two *words* have been run together (there is no space between them) then generally speaking pinpoint with the cursor where the space ought to be and *insert* a space, using the space bar.
6   Where two *lines* have been run together and you require a blank line between them (as between paragraphs) then generally speaking position the cursor where the blank line is to be, and *insert* a blank line, using the RETURN key, or its equivalent. If your system indicates by a symbol on the screen where a carriage return has been used, check to make sure that a carriage return symbol appears every time it is needed.

7   Where there are too many spaces between words, remember that a space counts as a character. Position the cursor where the unwanted space is and delete that space.

8   Where you have too many blank lines and want to close up the text, then position the cursor on the unwanted blank line and delete that line.

## Assignment 2

While keying in Assignment 2, keep an eye on the line and character numbers on the status line, if you have one. You have been asked to prepare a memorandum to go to all staff following a rather disastrous fire drill.

If your system requires you to give your document a name before you key it in, the suggested name is FIRE.

In this assignment you will:

–Key in text, using the wraparound facility.
–Divide the text into three paragraphs. The style is fully blocked.
–Correct any keying-in errors.
–Change a word and delete a word.
–Print out.

*Please follow these instructions:*

1   Key in the text as given, starting on line 4 of the screen. Type *continuously* if your system allows for this.

2   Correct your keying in errors.

3   Make the following amendments:
    –In paragraph 1 change Monday to Friday.
    –In paragraph 1 delete the word 'personal' from the phrase 'personal belongings'.

4   Make sure that the correct number of clear line spaces is left between paragraphs. On some systems it is necessary to insert a 'hard' space between the paragraphs. A 'hard', or 'protected' space is one which has been deliberately inserted by the operator to prevent words, sentences or paragraphs merging together when printed out. On some systems the space bar and carriage return key are sufficient to ensure this; on others, additional keys (such as a CONTROL key) have to be pressed.

**Assignment 2**
Handwritten notice

The fire drill which was carried out last Monday was not as successful as it should have been. Some members of staff were seen returning to their offices to collect coats and other personal belongings; windows and doors were left wide open in some rooms; some members of staff failed to report to their Fire Warden at the assembly point.

A further fire drill will, therefore, be held some time during next week. Would all members of staff please ensure that they adhere strictly to the instructions laid down.

The importance of following the correct procedures during fire drill cannot be too strongly emphasised. Failure to do so might result in loss of life if a real fire were to occur.

NRF

5　Identify your work by adding your initials, or some other reference, at the foot of the text. Use the SHIFT LOCK to do this.

6　Print out your document.

7　Check your work against the fair copy shown below. The line endings on your printout will not necessarily be the same as on the fair copy, depending on your pre-set margins and the print wheel used.

8　When you are satisfied that all is correct, you can delete your document (called FIRE) from the disk or the screen, as it will not be needed again.

**Text manipulation**　There are many instances where you will need not only to correct individual words, but also to manipulate the text in some way. For example, you may wish to delete whole words, phrases, sentences, paragraphs or pages. You may wish to centre headings, or underline words. You may wish to embolden headings, words or whole sentences.

**Assignment 2**
Fair copy

---

The fire drill which was carried out last Friday was not as successful as it should have been.  Some members of staff were seen returning to their offices to collect coats and other belongings; windows and doors were left wide open in some rooms; some members of staff failed to report to their Fire Warden at the assembly point.

A further fire drill will, therefore, be held some time during next week.  Would all members of staff please ensure that they adhere strictly to the instructions laid down.

The importance of following the correct procedures during fire drill cannot be too strongly emphasised.  Failure to do so might result in loss of life if a real fire were to occur.


NRF

---

*Emboldening* means that when the text is printed out, the characters which are emboldened will be printed in bolder type than the rest of the text. Some machines allow two densities of emboldening, others allow the printing to be white on black, rather than black on white. They are all means of emphasis which a specific machine may or may not allow you to use.

The different types of text manipulation are likely to be:

*Deleting* words, phrases, sentences, paragraphs, etc.
*Moving* words, phrases, sentences, paragraphs, etc.
*Inserting* words, phrases, sentences, paragraphs, etc.
*Centring* text
*Emboldening* text
*Underlining* text
*Converting* text into upper case
*Converting* text into lower case

Here again, the way in which this is done on each machine will vary greatly – emboldening, for example, is very easy on some machines, very complicated on others and on some it is not possible at all. However, the principles remain the same: the machine must know exactly *which* words, phrases, sentences, etc., you wish to underline, or move, or delete and you must pinpoint these, and then instruct the machine to carry out the required function.

So, the cursor is used to *pinpoint* the part of the text which is to be manipulated, the text is *highlighted* and the desired function *carried out*.

On some machines the text is literally highlighted – in other words it becomes more brilliant on the screen. On others, by pressing dedicated/named keys, the highlighting and carrying out are done in the same keystroke – keys called WORD DELETE or PARA DELETE, for example, highlight the text and carry out the deletion all at once.

Sometimes the instruction is given by pressing named keys, sometimes it is given by giving specific commands. The latter is an example of when a command is required *during* editing.

If, for exmple, a whole paragraph is to be moved from one part of the document to another, then once the paragraph to be moved has been pinpointed, the machine will need to be commanded to perform the move. These are *commands* concerned with getting the text right on the screen.

There are other commands, however, which have nothing to do with the editing and text manipulation processes, but are more to do with the storing or printing out of documents.

### STAGE 2    Storing or saving your work

This stage is concerned with storing the text in the computer's memory. Most terminals have a limited amount of temporary memory which will store a certain amount of text for a time, but which will disappear when the machine is switched off. It is therefore necessary to store the text more permanently, normally on disk. Some word processors still use a cassette tape as a storage medium, but this is rather cumbersome, and most data is stored on disk of one sort or another. The various types of storage media have been described more fully in Chapter 3.

Whatever the storage medium used, the WP must be instructed to save the text and store it for future use. Of course, the way to do this varies from machine to machine, but the most common commands used for this process are to SAVE the text or to WRITE it to disk. Sometimes there are special keys available to do this, but more often than not one of the QWERTY keys is used to perform this function.

Supposing, for example, you wished to store on disk the correct text of Assignment 2. Very often the key used to give an instruction to store or save work is 'S' (for SAVE) or 'W' (for WRITE) or 'A' (for ADD). If you have been keying in or correcting and amending the text, then just pressing the letter 'W' will make a 'W' appear on the screen somewhere in your text – which is *not* what you want. You have been editing, and are still in what is often called *edit mode*.

What you will need to do is to put the machine into *command mode*: you are going to process the document in some way, and you must tell the machine exactly what it is you are aiming to do. Getting into command mode usually means pressing a special function key, or a designated QWERTY key and a control key at the same time. Your instruction manual will tell you how to get the machine into the right mode for receiving commands.

Once the appropriate menu has appeared on the screen, or the machine indicates in some other way that it is ready to receive commands, the correct command can be given *and confirmed*.

It is usual to have to *confirm* a command in some way. This is normally done by pressing the ENTER or RETURN key or EXECUTE key. Most keyboards will have one or other of these keys – some will have two, or even all three, and you must press the right one for your particular machine.

So to give a command to save your text on disk you normally:

Make sure you are in command mode and/or the right menu is on the screen.
Give the appropriate command: often S or W, or A for saving or storing text on disk.
Confirm the command given by pressing RETURN or ENTER.

**STAGE 3   Recalling (for amendment) and/or printing out your work**
In Stage 1 you have keyed in text and got it right on the screen. In Stage 2 you have saved your work and stored it away, normally on disk. Now in Stage 3 you can either *recall* your work from disk back onto the screen for amendment, or *print it out*, or both.

Here again you will need to give specific commands to the machine, telling it exactly what you want it to do, and of course the commands will differ depending on your machine and your software.

Here the commands most commonly used give instructions:

To *read* a document (when there are no amendments to be made – you just wish to check what has been said).
To *re-write* or *modify* or *amend* text which you have recalled to the screen (when you have to make amendments).
To *print out* text either when it is on the screen or direct from the disk.

Your instruction manual will tell you which keys to press to give the commands you need. Obviously, there are many more things you will wish to do with your text, particularly in Stages 1 and 3, than have been described so far, and these are set out in the next chapter. However, let us look at the closing down procedures so that you can stop work at any time.

## Closing down

You should always try to leave a short amount of time at the end of the working day to carry out the correct closing down procedure. 'A short amount of time' can be up to fifteen minutes, depending on how much disk copying is needed, and how long the actual closing down procedure takes.

There are several things to be attended to at the end of the working session:

1 Deleting unwanted work,
2 Copying a document or disk,
3 Clearing away,
4 Closing down/logging off.

**1 Deleting unwanted work**
You will appreciate that, just as in any filing system, you only want to keep stored on disk work which you will need again. Certainly in the initial stages, when you are learning and trying out various pieces of work, you are unlikely to need to keep them all. At the end of the working session then, if you have not done so as you went along, it is a good discipline to assess the work you have done and see whether you want to retain it on disk or not. Disks can very easily get cluttered with unwanted work, and valuable storage space is lost.

To delete a document you normally have to:

1 Ensure that you are in command mode or the right command menu.
2 Give the correct command to delete the document (often 'D' or 'DD') and then the *name* of the document. You will often see this referred to in the manual as DOCNAME. The manual is asking you to key in the name you gave your document – absolutely accurately.
3 On most systems key in the number of the disk drive in which your disk is currently lodged. You must take care to see that this is right. If you do not, either the system will tell you that it cannot find your document on that disk or you will delete a document of the same name from the wrong disk.
4 Confirm that you do indeed wish to delete that particular document. This is where intelligent document naming can help – it is easy to delete a document by mistake if the document name means very little. For example RSB1 or RSB2 could be quite easily confused and the wrong document – containing, perhaps,

tens or hundreds of pages – inadvertently deleted. A document called HOOKBOOK (for a booklet by someone called Hook) or CONMEAD (for a contract with someone called MEAD) is less likely to be deleted by mistake, because the name itself describes the document to which it refers. Most systems ask you to confirm your command by pressing RETURN, ENTER or EXECUTE and then give you a choice to re-consider by asking ARE YOU SURE? or saying PRESS ENTER AGAIN TO CONFIRM, CANCEL TO ABORT, or some screen message in that vein. Take time to think for a moment before giving the final confirmation to delete an unwanted document.

## 2 Copying a document or disk

It is vital to make sure that you have copies of your work on spare disks in case your normal working disk is corrupted in any way. Procedures for ensuring this is done on a regular basis are more fully described in Chapter 7. Here is set down the *method* of making the system carry out the copying process.

Sometimes it is necessary to copy a single document from one disk to another, but more often a whole disk is copied – that is, all the documents on a disk are copied onto a second disk. Generally speaking the method will be:

1 Make sure that your backup disk is ready for you to copy on to – that it is formatted or initialized as a work disk and labelled, etc.
2 Ensure that you are in command mode or are on the right menu to start the disk copying process. This is called copying or duplicating, or security copying, or some other word which means 'copying'.
3 Give the correct commands to start the copying process, so that the system knows what you want to do.
4 When the final confirmation of the command is given, what will happen is that the system will copy onto the disk in one disk drive *whatever* is on the disk in the other disk drive. So, again it is imperative to make sure that you have got the right disks in the right disk drives.
5 Usually when the system is ready to copy, a screen message will say something like:

'Data on A1 will be overwritten by
data on A0. Press ENTER to confirm
or CANCEL to abort'

This means that the disk in drive A1 will become an exact copy of
the disk in drive A0, no matter what was on the disk in A1
before. So in this case you would need to put the disk you want
copied in drive A0, and the disk you want to copy onto in drive
A1. When you press ENTER the copying will take place.

6  It usually takes a few minutes to copy a disk, and while it is being
done screen messages will appear indicating which tracks on the
disk have been successfully copied. The messages will also
indicate where it has not been possible to copy because part of
the disk has been corrupted for some reason. (What to do if this
should happen is described more fully in Chapter 8.)

7  When the copying process has been completed, make sure you
are back in the right menu for shutting down the system or in the
command mode ready to do so.

8  Record that the disk has been copied, and the day and time on
which it was done.

### 3  Clearing away

If a manual catalogue of disks and documents (your filing index) is
kept, then this is the time of day when you can make sure it is up to
date, if you have not done so as you went along. It is the sort of job
you can do while the disk copying is in progress. You can also make
sure that disks are correctly stored away in the right place and that
printwheels, ribbons, stationery and any other materials are carefully and tidily put away. Naturally it is always sensible to work in a
tidy fashion, but with WP equipment and materials it is even more
important because they are expensive and can easily get bent, torn
or lost.

### 4  Closing down/logging off

As with switching on and getting started, every system will have its
own sequence of events for switching off, and this *must* be followed
if work is not to be lost or the system corrupted.

The general sequence for closing down is:

1  Make sure you have stored away on your disk the work you have
been doing.

2   Return to the main menu or the command mode. On large systems where perhaps you are linked to a mainframe, then follow the correct procedures for closing down your particular terminal. This is often called 'logging off'. *Never* just switch off your machine with work still on the screen unless your system specifically tells you to do so.

3   Remove and store away all the disks.

4   Switch off the terminal, the disk drive *and* the printer – in a specific order if told to do so.

5   Close the disk drives (if you are using floppy disks) so that less dust can get in.

6   Cover the machine – if it has a cover.

7   Switch off the power supply, if this is necessary for your particular system.

You should by now be able to:

1   Switch on, prepare your disks and load your programs.

2   Name your documents.

3   Interpret some screen messages.

4   Recognise whether you are giving commands or carrying out editing functions.

5   Recognise whether you are using a page-based or a document-based system, and move around the document accordingly.

6   Do some simple keying in and text corrections and manipulation.

7   Store your work on disk.

8   Print out your work.

9   Delete unwanted work from disk.

10  Copy disk if you wish.

11  Follow the closing down and switching off procedures.

In all these functions, you have seen that it is necessary to:

follow a sequence *exactly* – step by step,
think and act *logically*.

This applies equally to the functions described in the next chapter. It is always worth remembering that the machine will do exactly as it is told – no more and no less – and that you are in charge of it – not it of you.

# 6

# Gaining Experience

Once you have mastered the first steps in word processing –
switching and logging on and off, simple keying in and correction of
errors – you will wish to know how to perform various word
processing functions.

The assignments in this chapter are designed to let you practise
different functions, building on what you have already done. Naturally you will need to refer to your training and/or user manuals to
find out *how* to carry out these functions on your particular
machine. The assignments given here suggest *what* you should do,
not *how* you should do it. It may be that your machine will not allow
you to perform all the suggested functions.

Once you have completed all that you can do on each assignment,
check your work with the fair copy of the assignment. Again (as in
Assignment 2) the line endings will not necessarily be the same; this
is partly because the line lengths used as illustrations in a book do
not always equate with the line lengths you would find on a normal
A4 page.

## Assignment 3

The main purpose of this assignment is to allow you to practise
setting margins and printing your work in the right place on the
page. Margin setting is normally a simple operation, but has to be
done mathematically rather than using margin stops as you would

on a typewriter. Underlining and emboldening are also used, to enhance the appearance of the work. The functions which you will perform, as well as keying in, are:

–Setting margins
–Keying in different styles of heading
–Emboldening
–Underlining
–Printing out
–Right-hand justification

The background to the assignment is that the Office Manager wishes to send a notice about stationery to all members of staff, and to display the notice on the notice board. It is important, therefore, that it is well set out, as well as being accurate.

*Instructions*

1   Set document margins at 18 and 62 for a 12-pitch printwheel or 10 and 55 for a 10-pitch printwheel.
2   Key in the text as given. The heading STATIONERY should be on line 8.
3   Leave sufficient clear line spaces between headings, etc. to achieve a well-displayed notice.
4   Embolden the heading **STATIONERY**.
5   Underline the heading Notice to Staff.
6   Embolden the job title **Office Manager**.
7   Print out, with the right-hand margin justified if possible
8   Check your text for accuracy and appearance.
9   Correct any errors.
10  Adjust margins, etc., until the printout looks attractive.
11  Delete your document if not required again.
12  Compare your work with the fair copy illustrated.

**Assignment 3**
Handwritten notice

STATIONERY

<u>Notice to staff</u>

Unfortunately our regular supplier of stationery has suddenly gone out of business. Steps are promptly being taken to ensure a satisfactory supply of stationery, but negotiations with a new supplier may take a little time, and staff may find that certain items of stationery are out of stock for the time being.

Members of staff are asked to be particularly economical in their use of stationery and to be patient if the stationery they require is not immediately available. If special items of stationery are urgently required please let me know at once, and I will try to obtain emergency supplies.

Joan Price

Office Manager

**Assignment 3**
Fair copy

**STATIONERY**

Notice to Staff

Unfortunately   our   regular   supplier   of
stationery has suddenly gone out of business.
Steps are promptly being taken to ensure a
satisfactory   supply   of   stationery,   but
negotiations with a new supplier may take a
little time, and staff may find that certain
items of stationery are out of stock for the
time being.

Members of staff are asked to be particularly
economical in their use of stationery and to
be patient if the stationery they require is
not immediately available. If special items
of stationery are urgently required, please
let me know at once, and I will try to obtain
emergency supplies.

Joan Price
**Office Manager**

## Assignment 4

Tab setting, like margin setting, is usually fairly easy, once the places of the tab settings have been worked out. You need to work out *where* to put the tab, just as you would do on a typewriter. In this assignment you will find that this has been done for you.

In this assignment ordinary tabs are used, rather than decimal tabs or centre tabs – these will be used in a later assignment.

What you will find much easier on the word processor than on a typewriter, is to alter the tabs and tabulated work once it has been keyed in.

In this assignment, then, you will:

–Set margins
–Set tabs
–Key in tabulated work
–Alter the tab settings
–Print out
–Store the work on disk and retain it

The car parking list of any office requires constant updating, (internal telephone lists come into the same category). So in this assignment you practise getting the list onto disk and retaining it for future amendment. The suggested document name is CARS.

**Assignment 4**
Handwritten list

CAR PARKING

Car parking spaces have been allocated as follows:

| Parking Space | Name | Car Registration Number |
|---|---|---|
| 01 | Miss V Barnet | WL 1 |
| 02 | Mr B Dacey | C460 KUW |
| 03 | Mr. D. Saunders | C 323 PWV |
| 04 | Mr F. Marsden | C 324 PWV |
| 05 | Mr K. Baxter | C 325 PWV |
| 06 | Mrs M. Downs | B 505 WHV |
| 07 | Miss E. Baker | MUC 623W |
| 08 | Ms. M. Frampton | A405 TVA |
| 09 | Mr. C. Loader | BFP 231X |
| 10 | Mr. D. Waters | CUU 420S |

Double spacing please

*Instructions*

1   Set document margins at 5 and 75 for 12 pitch printwheel and 1
    and 70 for 10 pitch printwheel.
2   Set tabs at 22 and 45 for 12 pitch and 20 and 40 for 10 pitch.
3   Key in the text, making your own judgement on emboldening
    and underlining. Block each column at the tab setting.
4   Make sure that the list itself is in double spacing.
5   Check the text for accuracy and appearance.
6   Alter the tab settings to 25 and 50 for 12 pitch and 23 and 45 for
    10 pitch, to give better spacing between the columns, and
    re-align the text.
7   Shorten the third column heading (Car Registration Number)
    by deleting the word 'Car'. Make sure any underlining or
    emboldening is still correct.
8   Print out the list.
9   Check your work for accuracy and appearance, and amend as
    necessary.
10  Important – save your work on the disk. Do *not* delete it.
11  Check your list with the fair copy, and make sure your screen is
    clear or that you are back in command mode.

**Assignment 4**
Fair copy

**CAR PARKING**

Car parking spaces have been allocated as follows:

| Parking Space | Name | Registration Number |
| --- | --- | --- |
| 01 | Miss V Barnet | WL 1 |
| 02 | Mr B Dacey | C460 KUW |
| 03 | Mr D Saunders | C323 PWV |
| 04 | Mr F Marsden | C324 PWV |
| 05 | Mr K Baxter | C325 PWV |
| 06 | Mrs M Downs | B505 WHV |
| 07 | Miss E Baker | MUC 623W |
| 08 | Ms M Frampton | A405 TVA |
| 09 | Mr C Loader | BFP 231X |
| 10 | Mr D Waters | CUU 420S |

## Assignment 5

This is a good exercise for showing how quickly amendments and printouts can be made once the initial keying in has been done and the format of the document established.

In this assignment you will:

–Recall a document from disk
–Make a quick amendment
–Print out the amended version
–Save the *amended* version

The background is that one of the company representatives has left and is to be replaced by a Mr Cathcart. Mr Cathcart will be taking over Mr Saunders' car and his parking space – the car parking list needs amending accordingly. Please save the *amended* version on the disk: the original version is no longer applicable. You may wish to make a note of the date of the amendment on the disk and on the printout.

*Instructions*

1  Recall the car parking list (Assignment 4) from the disk, ready for amendment.
2  Alter 'Mr D Saunders' to 'Mr M Cathcart'.
3  Add the amendment date at the bottom of the page.
4  Print out the amended version.
5  Save the *amended* version on the disk.

**Assignment 5**
Amended list

---

**CAR PARKING**

Car parking spaces have been allocated as follows:

| Parking Space | Name | Registration Number |
|---|---|---|
| 01 | Miss V Barnet | WL 1 |
| 02 | Mr B Dacey | C460 KUW |
| 03 | Mr M Cathcart | C323 PWV |
| 04 | Mr F Marsden | C324 PWV |
| 05 | Mr K Baxter | C325 PWV |
| U6 | Mrs M Downs | B505 WHV |
| 07 | Miss E Baker | MUC 623W |
| 08 | Ms M Frampton | A405 TVA |
| 09 | Mr C Loader | BFP 231X |
| 10 | Mr D Waters | CUU 420S |

Amended 6 February 1986

## Assignment 6

The main objective of this assignment is to practise keying in an indented paragraph. Functions already used – margins, tabs, emboldening, etc. – are also used.

The assignment is in three parts:

1 Keying in the original letter and writing it to disk.
2 Making a substantial amendment to the letter and altering the format accordingly.
3 Printing out an accompanying envelope or label.

During the course of this assignment you will:

–Set margins
–Set tabs
–Embolden and underline
–Centre
–Key in an indented paragraph
–Print out using headed paper
–Write to disk
–Recall from disk and amend
–Delete a paragraph
–Alter margins
–Print an envelope or label

Your department has received a letter of complaint about a 'Carryall' shopping bag. The Marketing Manager suspects that there may be similar complaints, so you will be writing to the complainant and keeping a copy of the letter on disk.

**Assignment 6**
Handwritten letter

Miss Edwina Brown
20 Elmbank Road
Hertford
Herts

(Date)

Dear Miss Brown

CARRYALL SHOPPING BAG

Thank you very much for your letter which we received this morning. I am very sorry to hear that the stitching on the handle of your CARRYALL shopping bag appears to be faulty.

I note from your letter that you purchased the bag at your local Superstore more than a year ago. I should like to point out that it is policy of the company is

*Embolden* that goods found to be unsatisfactory (within six months) of purchase will be replaced immediately, or credit given for the sum involved.

However, since it is obvious from your letter that your CARRYALL bag has been little used during the past year, I have pleasure in enclosing a replacement.

I regret that I am not able to supply you with a blue CARRYALL shopping bag, as this colour has now been discontinued. I hope that you will find the brown one to your liking.

Yours sincerely

(Mrs) Mary Warner
(Marketing Manager) — Embolden

*Instructions*

*Part 1*

1   Key in the letter to Miss Brown, setting margins at 12 and 68 (12 pitch) or 5 and 65 (10 pitch).
2   Set the tab for the indented paragraph at 18 (12 pitch) or 10 (10 pitch). This could be called, on your machine, the temporary margin or autotab function, or something similar.
3   Embolden, underline or centre as indicated.
4   Print out using headed paper.
5   Save the letter on disk – suggested document name: CARRYALL.

*Part 2*

Your Marketing Manager has discovered that there *is* a blue bag she can send after all, so she wants you to delete the last paragraph.

1   Recall letter to screen.
2   Delete final paragraph.
3   Alter margins to 15 and 65 (12 pitch) or 10 and 60 (10 pitch) to take account of the shorter letter.
4   Indent the paragraph at 20 (12 pitch) or 15 (10 pitch) and alter the right-hand margin of the indented paragraph to 55 (12 pitch) or 50 (10 pitch).
5   Print out the amended letter.
6   Save the amended letter on disk.

*Part 3*

You have suddenly remembered that you should have supplied your packing department with a label addressed to Miss Brown. It is important that this is done quickly.

1   Recall the letter to the screen as quickly as possible.
2   Print out a label or an envelope using the quickest method possible.

*Note:*   On some systems it may be necessary to re-key the name and address in order to print out.

**Assignment 6**
Fair copy

# D L Cases Ltd

Unit 64
Elvester Industrial Estate
COPTHORPE
Warwicks

Miss Edwina Brown
20 Elmbank Road
Hertford
Herts

8 March 1986

Dear Miss Brown

**CARRYALL SHOPPING BAG**

Thank you very much for your letter which we received this
morning.  I am very sorry to hear that the stitching on the
handle of your CARRYALL shopping bag appears to be faulty.

I note from your letter that you purchased the bag at your
local Superstore more than a year ago.  I should like to
point out that the policy of the company is:

> that goods found to be unsatisfactory
> **within six months** of purchase will
> be replaced immediately, or credit
> given for the sum involved.

However, since it is obvious from your letter that your
CARRYALL bag has been little used during the past year, I
have pleasure in enclosing a replacement.

Yours sincerely

(Mrs) Mary Warner
**Marketing Manager**

Enclosure

## Assignment 7

The relationship between the word processor and the photocopier can be well illustrated by positioning two A5 pieces of work on an A4 sheet, ready for photocopying and guillotining. This assignment is an invitation which needs to be reproduced exactly in the two halves of an A4 sheet. This gives good practice in centring, layout, compensating for lines inserted and deleted, and temporary storage and retrieval of text.

In this assignment you will:

–Centre several lines of text
–Use the flush right facility where this is available
–Store the work in a temporary/scratch file or use the cut and leave facility

You have been asked, as a favour, to produce the invitation to Mr Carter's farewell party. You decide to do two copies on one sheet of A4 paper.

**Assignment 7**
Handwritten draft

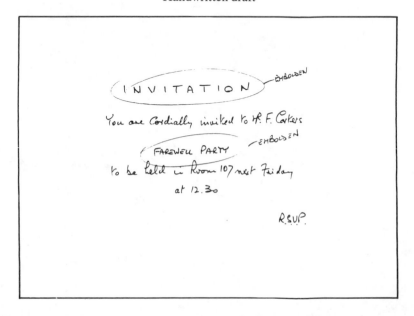

*Instructions*

1   Use margins and spacing at your own discretion to lay the invitation out on half an A4 sheet.
2   Key in the invitation, centring each line except RSVP.
3   Make sure that RSVP is flush against the right-hand margin. You may be able to use a decimal tab or flush-right facility for this.
4   Embolden as indicated.
5   Check your work for accuracy and appearance.
6   When you are satisfied with it, store all the invitation on a temporary file (scratch file, perhaps, or cut and leave, copy block, etc. according to the system you are using) and reproduce it at the bottom of the page.
7   Print out the invitation on A4. Fold the A4 sheet in half horizontally to test whether both copies of the invitation are correctly positioned.
8   Correct and/or adjust your text as necessary and print out until you are satisfied with the result.

**Assignment 7**
Fair copy

I N V I T A T I O N

You are cordially invited to Mr F Carter's

**FAREWELL PARTY**

to be held in Room 107 next Friday

at 12 30

RSVP

- - - - - - - - - - - - - - - - - - - - - - - - - - - - - - - - -

I N V I T A T I O N

You are cordially invited to Mr F Carter's

**FAREWELL PARTY**

to be held in Room 107 next Friday

at 12 30

RSVP

## Assignment 8

One of the things anyone working with a word processor often has to do is to amend and print out work prepared by other people. It is obviously not possible for you to have the text of this assignment pre-stored on your own disk, which means that you will have to key in the work, which is rather a long job.

The assignment is given here as an amended draft on hard copy. Obviously you will wish to make some of the alterations as you go along – you may well make mistakes yourself, which will need correcting.

The main aim of this assignment is to practise moving text from one page to another and to perform the SEARCH and REPLACE function. It also enables you to print from background and to use the automatic page numbering facility, if you have it.

In this assignment you will:

–Key in a lengthy document
–Move text
–Search and replace
–Print from background giving appropriate print directives
–Number the pages automatically

Although the draft is in 1½ spacing, the final printout will be in single spacing – you should take this into account as you key in the text. The final printout should be:

–on A4 paper
–in single spacing
–12 pitch
–right-hand justified
–numbered at the bottom of each page in the centre

**Assignment 8**
Amended draft

---

ASSIGNMENT NO 8

'OUR LIVELIHOOD DEPENDS'
→ Centre

Please change
"customers" to
"CUSTOMERS"
throughout the document

DRAFT

**TRAINING NOTES**
→ Centre

PREFACE

These training notes, which highlight the main points covered by the audio visual programme, are designed to provide a framework for the course leader to build a specific session, based on some or all aspects covered.

The course leader should interpret these notes in the way most suitable to the objectives of the session and to his/her own style of presentation.

The audio visual programme itself should be considered as an **aid** rather than an end in itslef.

1   INTRODUCTION

Sometimes when we go shopping we're faced with examples of something less than good customer service.  What are our feelings in that kind of situation?  Do we feel we want to go back to those places the next time we need to shop? Very likely not.  Could it be that customers sometimes have the same reaction when they come into our branches?

Amended draft – *cont.*

---

2  CUSTOMERS ARE NECESSARY

Let's consider a very basic question.  'Why do we need customers at
all?'  The answer to that can be summed up as follows: we need
customers because our livelihood depends upon them.  Without them we
have no jobs.

So, customers are the most important people who come into our shops
and stores.  To be frank, without customers there would be no reason
to employ sales assistants, checkout operators, shefl filllers,
section managers, supervisors, or even head office people.

So, your pay, your job, your progress within the organisation depends
upon whether customers are satisfied with the service they receive
when they come into our branches.  Our policy is that customers are
important people without whom we, as a business, could not survive.

3  APPEARANCE AND ATTITUDE

Be aware of the impression you're giving to a cukstomer by the way you
stand, look and so on.  Attitude isnf't only to do with speaking.

*Run on*

Know about changes in your stock, whether it be the range,
specifications, sizes or price.  Be prepared to explain these politely
to customers.

Sometimes customers are fussy; indeed they can be rude on occasions.
Whatever you feel inside, always make sure thjat your appearance and
attitude is beyond reproach.

Amended draft – *cont.*

It's possible to become tired of customers repeatedly asking the same
questions. Remember the question is important to the customer and it
must be answered pleasantly and courteously. Don't forget, if you're
not sure of the answer, find out. Don't guess, you might be wrong.

In self service departments the stock is there for customers to pick
up or not as they please. While to a certain extent that's true, you
have a duty to be helpful to customers who approach you. It **is** part
of your job to be of assistance.

There are always customers who come in at the last moment, just on
closing time and expect you to spend time showing them what they want.
Attitude in this situation is very important. They are customers and
mustn't be made to feel unwelcome. The fact that they have come into
our store rather than our competitor's, should be reason enough to
make them feel welcome.

4  ATTITUDES WITHIN THE ORGANISATION

It's important that the right attitude exists between departments
**within** the organisation.  We all belong to the same organisation, so
give all the help you can to your colleagues.

Head Office

Remember that branches are important customers to you.  Without
the branches to stimulate every aspect of the business, we
wouldn't need a Head Office.  So, if a branch wants information
about an item of stock, remember it's important to that branch
and there's a particular reason for asking.

*Move to below "Branch" para at Ⓐ*

Amended draft – *cont.*

Branches

Head Office is there to support you.  This can't be done
effectively if the attitude between you in wrong.  If Head
Office asks for specific information or for the return of
documents by a certain time, remember there's a purpose behind
it, and respond positively.  If for some good reason it's
unrealistic, say so - courteously.

Ⓐ → Put "Head Office" para in here

( Back up/Service Departments ) — Underlined, not
emboldened

The attitude you adopt in your dealings with both Head Office
and branches must be the same as that we're expecting the
branches to adopt towards our customers.

Bear in mind that good customer service, whether direct or indirect,
increases sales and we should all be working together towards the same
end: satisfying our customers.


5  CONCLUSION

As a business organisation, we need the turnover our customers
provide.  Losing a customer means a loss of income and a loss of
(income) must eventually mean a loss of jobs somewhere along the line.
  ` not emboldened

We need customers in order to remain in business.  Without customers
we have no jobs.  So, customers are essential to us.  Our livelihood
depends upon them, never lose sight of that fact.

─────────────

**Assignment 8**
Corrected printout

---

'OUR LIVELIHOOD DEPENDS'

**TRAINING NOTES**

<u>PREFACE</u>

These training notes, which highlight the main points covered by the audio visual programme, are designed to provide a framework for the course leader to build a specific session, based on some or all aspects covered.

The course leader should interpret these notes in the way most suitable to the objectives of the session and to his/her own style of presentation.

The audio visual programme itself should be considered as an **aid** rather than an end in itself.

<u>1  INTRODUCTION</u>

Sometimes when we go shopping we're faced with examples of something less than good customer service.  What are our feelings in that kind of situation?  Do we feel we want to go back to those places the next time we need to shop? Very likely not.  Could it be that CUSTOMERS sometimes have the same reaction when they come into our branches?

<u>2  CUSTOMERS ARE NECESSARY</u>

Let's consider a very basic question.  'Why do we need CUSTOMERS at all?'  The answer to that can be summed up as follows:  we need CUSTOMERS because our livelihood depends upon them.  Without them we have no jobs.

So, CUSTOMERS are the most important people who come into our shops and stores.  To be frank, without CUSTOMERS there would be no reason to employ sales assistants, checkout operators, shelf fillers, section managers, supervisors, or even head office people.

- 1 -

Corrected printout – *cont.*

So, your pay, your job, your progress within the organisation depends upon whether CUSTOMERS are satisfied with the service they receive when they come into our branches. Our policy is that CUSTOMERS are important people without whom we, as a business, could not survive.

## 3  APPEARANCE AND ATTITUDE

Be aware of the impression you're giving to a customer by the way you stand, look and so on. Attitude isn't only to do with speaking. Know about changes in your stock, whether it be the range, specifications, sizes or price. Be prepared to explain these politely to CUSTOMERS.

Sometimes CUSTOMERS are fussy; indeed they can be rude on occasions. Whatever you feel inside, always make sure that your appearance and attitude is beyond reproach.

It's possible to become tired of CUSTOMERS repeatedly asking the same questions. Remember the question is important to the customer and it must be answered pleasantly and courteously. Don't forget, if you're not sure of the answer, find out. Don't guess, you might be wrong.

In self service departments the stock is there for CUSTOMERS to pick up or not as they please. While to a certain extent that's true, you have a duty to be helpful to CUSTOMERS who approach you. It **is** part of your job to be of assistance.

There are always CUSTOMERS who come in at the last moment, just on closing time and expect you to spend time showing them what they want. Attitude in this situation is very important. They are CUSTOMERS and mustn't be made to feel unwelcome. The fact that they have come into our store rather than our competitor's, should be reason enough to make them feel welcome.

## 4  ATTITUDES WITHIN THE ORGANISATION

It's important that the right attitude exists between departments **within** the organisation. We all belong to the same organisation, so give all the help you can to your colleagues.

- 2 -

Corrected printout – *cont.*

---

### Branches

Head Office is there to support you. This can't be done effectively if the attitude between you is wrong. If Head Office asks for specific information or for the return of documents by a certain time, remember there's a purpose behind it, and respond positively. If for some good reason it's unrealistic, say so - courteously.

### Head Office

Remember that branches are important CUSTOMERS to you. Without the branches to stimulate every aspect of the business, we wouldn't need a Head Office. So, if a branch wants information about an item of stock, remember it's important to that branch and there's a particular reason for asking.

### Back up/Service Departments

The attitude you adopt in your dealings with both Head Office and branches must be the same as that we're expecting the branches to adopt towards our CUSTOMERS.

Bear in mind that good customer service, whether direct or indirect, increases sales and we should all be working together towards the same end: satisfying our CUSTOMERS.

### 5 CONCLUSION

As a business organisation, we need the turnover our CUSTOMERS provide. Losing a customer means a loss of income and a loss of income **must** eventually mean a loss of jobs somewhere along the line.

We need CUSTOMERS in order to remain in business. Without CUSTOMERS we have no jobs. So, CUSTOMERS are essential to us. Our livelihood depends upon them, never lose sight of that fact.

---

- 3 -

## Assignment 9

One of the most frequent applications of word processing is the form letter or mail merge/list processing function. This assignment lets you practise this for only three letters, but the principle will be the same for any number.

The assignment can be dealt with in two ways:

1   As a form letter, where you key in a standard letter marked where the variables will appear. You recall this to the screen the required number of times and infill the variables as necessary.
2   As a mail merge or list processing exercise. You key in the same letter, marking where the variables will appear, *but* according to the mail merge format of your system. You then create a separate document with the names and addresses, and merge the two documents together.

Choose one of these methods according to your system and its capabilities. Method 1 is probably easier, although not necessarily so.

## Assignment 9
Standard letter

(Today's date)

*

Dear *

**SALES MANAGER**

Thank you very much for attending the interview for the above position last *. I very much regret that, on this occasion, you were unsuccessful in your application.

As you know, the response to our advertisement for this position was very heavy, and many applicants were of a very high calibre indeed. We shall keep your details on our files and contact you again should a similar vacancy arise within the company.

Yours sincerely

David Pritchard
**Personnel Director**

Please send to:

1. E. A. James Esq
   21 Willow Way
   Bromley. Kent
       Interview Day   Wednesday

2. Miss K. Parsons
   43 Chester Street
   Huddersfield, Yorks
       Interview Day  Thursday

3. W Robertson Esq
   134 Kingston Avenue
   Surbiton, Surrey
       Interview Day  Thursday

**Assignment 9**
Standard letter with infilled variables

# WENLOCKS Plc

Wenlock House   113 Station Road
BRATLEY                    Surrey

15 December 1985

E A James Esq
21 Willow Way
BROMLEY
Kent

Dear Mr James

**SALES MANAGER**

Thank you very much for attending the interview for the above position
last WEDNESDAY.  I very much regret that, on this occasion, you were
unsuccessful in your application.

As you know, the response to our advertisement for this position was
very heavy, and many applicants were of a very high calibre indeed.
We shall keep your details on our files and contact you again should a
similar vacancy arise within the company.

Yours sincerely

David Pritchard
**Personnel Director**

## Assignment 10

Documents often need to be produced in landscape rather than portrait form, and for this the wide screen facility must be used. The assignment is also a good opportunity to try using different forms of tab setting and to practise again the temporary storage and recall of a format – in this case the headings before the figures are keyed in. You will find that it takes a long time to set up the format, but once set it is easy to use. You will also experience text appearing on the right and disappearing off the left-hand side of the screen.

In this assignment you will:

–Use wide screen/horizontal scroll
–Use various tab settings:
    ordinary tabs
    centre tabs
    decimal tabs
–Store headings in temporary storage for use further down the page
–Use vertical lines if you have this facility

The Accounts Department has been asked to provide figures for January and February, showing the amounts owed to the Company by two customers – P. K. Holdings Ltd and David Evans & Co Ltd. You will have to create the headings and infill the appropriate figures.

**Assignment 10**
Draft copy

Customer (Sales) Account

Customer's Name: P.K. HOLDINGS LTD
Reference No: A1405

As at: 28/02/86

| Invoice Date | Invoice Number | Net £ | VAT £ | Total £ | Payment Date | Payment Amount £ | Balance Outstanding £ |
|---|---|---|---|---|---|---|---|
| 09/01/86 | 1024 | 169.00 | 25.00 | 194.00 | | | 1166.44 |
| | | | | | | | 194.00 |
| 12/02/86 | 1025 | 78.44 | 11.17 | 90.21 | 02/02/86 | 972.44 | 284.21 |

Customer's Name: DAVID EVANS & Co LTD
Reference No: B2067

As at: 28/02/86

| Invoice Date | Invoice Number | Net £ | VAT £ | Total £ | Payment Date | Payment Amount £ | Balance Outstanding £ |
|---|---|---|---|---|---|---|---|
| 12/01/86 | 1534 | 5.51 | 0.83 | 6.34 | | | 1262.78 |
| 16/01/86 | 1535 | 36.37 | 5.50 | 42.17 | | | 1304.95 |
| 28/01/86 | 1536 | 267.86 | 40.18 | 308.04 | | | 1612.99 |

*Instructions*

1   If wide screen is to be used, call up this facility.
2   Margins are at 0 and 132 (12 pitch) or 0 and 120 (10 pitch).
3   Key in headings as shown:
     Main heading centred
     'Customer's Name', 'Reference No' at left margin
     'As at' (+ date) flush on right margin
4   Lines (vertical and horizontal) can be created on the screen or hand-ruled at a later stage, depending on the facilities available.
5   Column headings should be centred over each column. If a centre tab facility is available, then these should be set at: 12 pitch – 8, 24, 40, 56, 72, 91, 96, 101, 120 (the heading 'Payment' will be on the centre tab setting 96); 10 pitch – 8, 24, 37, 50, 65, 74, 80, 86, 102 (the heading 'Payment' will be on the centre tab setting 80).
6   Set ordinary tabs and decimal tabs for the data. (Decimal tabs should be used for the columns which contain amounts of money.)
     12 pitch – ordinary tabs at 4, 21 and 89
                     decimal tabs at 40, 56, 72, 101 and 120
     10 pitch – ordinary tabs at 4, 22 and 72
                     decimal tabs at 37, 50, 65, 86 and 102
7   Once the headings and tabs are set, save these (except for the main heading) in a temporary (scratch) file if possible, to use again further down the page.
8   Recall the headings and tabs into the second half of the page before keying in the data.
9   Key in the data as shown for the two customers. Print out, check and amend. Exit from wide screen if necessary.

**Assignment 10**
Fair copy

ASSIGNMENT NO 10

Customer (Sales) Account

Customer's Name: P. K. Holdings Ltd
Reference No: A1405

As at: 28/02/86

| Invoice Date | Invoice Number | Net £ | VAT £ | Total £ | Payment Date | Payment Amount £ | Balance Outstanding £ |
|---|---|---|---|---|---|---|---|
| 09/01/86 | 1024 | 169.00 | 25.00 | 194.00 | | | 1166.44 |
| 12/02/86 | 1025 | 78.44 | 11.17 | 90.21 | 02/02/86 | 972.44 | 194.00 |
| | | | | | | | 284.21 |

Customer's Name: David Evans & Co Ltd
Reference No: B2067

As at: 28/02/86

| Invoice Date | Invoice Number | Net £ | VAT £ | Total £ | Payment Date | Payment Amount £ | Balance Outstanding £ |
|---|---|---|---|---|---|---|---|
| 12/01/86 | 1534 | 5.51 | 0.83 | 6.34 | | | 1262.78 |
| 16/01/86 | 1535 | 36.37 | 5.50 | 42.17 | | | 1304.95 |
| 28/01/86 | 1536 | 267.86 | 40.18 | 308.04 | | | 1612.99 |

## Assignment 11

The *double column* facility is very useful for certain types of WP work. Some machines allow you to work independently on more than two columns, but they are usually the more powerful systems. Each column is an entity in itself in which you can correct, move text, underline and justify as you wish without disturbing the other column.

In this case the facility is used for an amateur dramatic society newsletter and gives scope for good layout and pleasing presentation.

There are certain to be definite rules which you have to follow on your machine to set up the two columns. These should be studied first and practised with this assignment.

The two columns do not *have* to be of equal width, but in this case they should be.

**Assignment 11**
Basic two-column layout

---

**'PRESENT LAUGHTER'**

by Noel Coward

After spending a happy evening watching 'Present Laughter' performed at the Greenwich Theatre, I decided that I should like to produce the play for our own audience and was delighted when the Committee agreed to allow me to do so.

It is a courageous actor who takes on the role performed by 'the Master' himself and I am very pleased - so far! - with **all** the cast. I am sure this is a production which our audience will enjoy.

Please do your best to sell as many tickets as you can - tell your friends that we shall, indeed, 'present laughter', and get them to come along and laugh with us.

**Producer**

remember remember remember

ANNUAL GENERAL MEETING

4 May 1986

remember remember remember

Thanks to all those who have sent in Noel Coward reminiscences so far - more please.

**Stage Manager**

remember remember remember

ANNUAL GENERAL MEETING

4 May 1986

remember remember remember

**SOUND TECHNICIAN**

'Present Laughter' will be Michael's 50th production with the Society. He started in 1968 with 'Isabel' and has provided the sound for every production since then - a steady and steadfast reliability which few of us could match.

So this short piece is to say a big thank you to Michael for the many, many hours of work he has put in and the splendid results he achieves.

**Chairman**

*Instructions*

1 Set the column widths at 0–38 and 42–80.
2 Key in the text in column A.
3 Centre the 'remember remember' lines within the column.
4 Save in the temporary storage the Annual General Meeting reminder in column A, since this is repeated in column B.
5 Key in the text in column B, recalling the AGM notice from temporary storage.
6 Make amendments to text and adjustments to layout as necessary.
7 Print out.
8 Add decoration by hand, as desired, to highlight the AGM reminders.
9 Exit from double column.

**Assignment 11**
Decorated two-column layout

### 'PRESENT LAUGHTER'

#### by Noel Coward

After spending a happy evening watching 'Present Laughter' performed at the Greenwich Theatre, I decided that I should like to produce the play for our own audience and was delighted when the Committee agreed to allow me to do so.

It is a courageous actor who takes on the role performed by 'the Master' himself and I am very pleased - so far! - with **all** the cast. I am sure this is a production which our audience will enjoy.

Please do your best to sell as many tickets as you can - tell your friends that we shall, indeed, 'present laughter', and get them to come along and laugh with us.

**Producer**

remember remember remember

ANNUAL GENERAL MEETING

4 May 1986

remember remember remember

Thanks to all those who have sent in Noel Coward reminiscences so far - more please.

**Stage Manager**

remember remember remember

ANNUAL GENERAL MEETING

4 May 1986

remember remember remember

#### SOUND TECHNICIAN

'Present Laughter' will be Michael's 50th production with the Society. He started in 1968 with 'Isabel' and has provided the sound for every production since then - a steady and steadfast reliability which few of us could match.

So this short piece is to say a big thank you to Michael for the many, many hours of work he has put in and the splendid results he achieves.

**Chairman**

# 7

# Managing the WP System

Whatever the size of your word processing system, unless it is properly 'managed', then a great deal of the benefits of speed and efficiency which a WP system can bring will be lost. Suppose that your hardware and software are right for the job they are required to do, that the operation of the machine is being done to a high standard, that the environment is right and that the quality of the input is good – yet, without good management the system will not be as effective as it should.

System management covers *office procedures* and *housekeeping procedures* which must be set up and maintained if the system is to run smoothly. When a new WP system is introduced into a working environment, the tendency is to let the procedures 'grow', instead of controlling them from the start. This is partly because people new to word processing are not aware of the procedures and disciplines which will be necessary. This chapter is intended to help the new user to establish these procedures, although naturally each place of work will require its individual interpretation of the suggestions made here.

It is immaterial whether your WP system is attached to a large mainframe computer, or whether it is a WP package which can be used on a desk-top micro – an efficient working routine must be set up and maintained. It is true that some aspects of the procedures may need to be altered in the light of experience. It is also true that setting up procedures and routines is a time-consuming business. It is false economy, however, not to devote the time required not only to setting up the procedures, but also to ensuring that everyone concerned with the routines and disciplines is trained in their use.

If you are a user setting up a system for yourself and other people to operate, then plan time for preparing your system management procedures and take the time to implement those plans properly – it pays off in the end.

If you are a new user setting up entirely for yourself, then it is very tempting to think that you will remember everything and not take the time to set up and maintain procedures for you, yourself to follow. Time taken disciplining yourself in this way, however, is not wasted.

If you are a new user joining a team of people who already have well-established procedures, then the message is that you must follow the procedures assiduously and accurately until you are sufficiently competent to make suggestions for their improvement.

The topics which this chapter will cover under the two main headings are:

*Office procedures*

1   Switching/logging on and off.
2   Document naming, indexing and filing.
3   Disk care and management.
4   Care and use of stationery and materials.
5   Workflow procedures.
6   Security.

*Housekeeping procedures*

1   Disk copying.
2   Controlling the disk space.
3   Disasters.

## Office procedures

### 1   Switching/logging on and off
Chapter 5 described in outline the principles of switching on and off correctly, and emphasised the need to follow instructions precisely so that work should not be lost, nor disks corrupted.

On a one-person operation this routine is not likely to be followed incorrectly. Where more than one person is using the system, however, it is essential to make sure that *everyone* knows the routine for this operation.

Switching on routines should be displayed near the central processing unit in larger systems, or be readily available to users on standalone systems. It is advisable to set these routines down on a piece of card, duly laminated or protected in some other way, so that the occasional user can switch on and get the system up and running (booted) without having to wait for the regular user to appear. It is better to have these instructions written out separately than to ask new and occasional users to find them in the operating manual.

A typical set of instructions for switching on a small, standalone system would be:

(NAME OF SYSTEM)
## SWITCHING ON ROUTINE

1 Switch on at wall socket.
2 Switch on VDU, disk drive and printer.
3 Put System Disk in Disk Drive $\emptyset$.
4 Press F4 key.
5 Main menu will appear on screen.
6 Load WP program: Key in 'W' and press ENTER.
7 Wait. LOADING message will appear on screen.
8 When loading is complete, system is ready.
9 Put required Work Disk in Disk Drive 1.

When writing instructions such as these it is important to set down the steps in order and start with a verb when the operator has to *do* something.

For larger systems the routine might be more complicated and it might be essential for the control of workflow purposes that users enter the date and precise time of switching or logging on. In this case then obviously the need for such accuracy would be highlighted in the instructions.

Switching/logging off routines can be treated similarly, but it is particularly important on larger, shared-logic systems that each user knows what is to be done. Work on several screens could be lost if an operator at the Central Processing Unit switched off without first checking that each workstation had been returned to the main logging off menu. Usually, dispersed systems have terminals located in different parts of the building, though tied to a central processor – in this case the operator at the central unit would have to check via the screen facility rather than walking round the building that individual terminals were closed down.

It seems to some people wasteful of electricity to leave a computer running all day, but in fact it makes better sense to leave it on, rather than risk losing work which would afterwards have to be re-keyed. The amount of electricity used by a computer is in fact quite small compared with other electrical appliances.

The questions to ask oneself about switching on and off processes are:

1   Is the procedure clear, correct and readily available?
2   Do all who need to know, know?
3   Can they easily find out?

## 2   Document naming, indexing and filing

Much has been said in Chapter 5 about the advisability of naming documents in an intelligent way and of using the facilities allowed for description and dating. If you are working on your own and nobody else ever needs to have access to your disks, then the naming of your documents can be a purely personal choice.

If, however, you are working with several other people, then it is as well to have a system for naming documents that each operator should follow. Obviously each place of work will devise a system which works for itself, but just as in any other filing system, it must be understood and followed by all. More time is lost in a WP environment trying to find a document that someone else has filed away somewhere than many people realise. You cannot, as in the days of typewriters and hard copy, go through a person's in-tray or filing cabinet and see at a glance which documents are where. The contents of a disk remain hidden unless a careful naming, indexing and filing system is maintained.

**Document naming**   As far as this is concerned, then, it is possible to devise a system where the operator must take as a document name the next name available under a certain heading. If, for example, a school or college divided its WP work into subject headings, then a catalogue could be drawn up under those headings, document names allocated, and the operator required to use the next free name. Fig. 7.1 shows an example of how this would work.

| DATE | DOCNAME | DESCRIPTION | NO OF PAGES | OPERATOR | DATE DELETED |
|------|---------|-------------|-------------|----------|--------------|
| 12/02 | SPELL.1 | Plural exercise | 4 | DW | |
| 13/02 | SPELL.2 | Apostrophes | 3 | DW | |
| 14/03 | SPELL.3 | Commonly mis-spelled words | 6 | VH | |
| | SPELL.4 | | | | |
| | SPELL.5 | | | | |

**Fig. 7.1**

In this example the column headed DOCNAME would be pre-typed. When an operator came to key in the next document concerned with English spelling, then the next DOCNAME available (SPELL.4) would be used, and the various details added to the catalogue. Other operators or tutors would then be able to look up at a later date under the general heading ENGLISH SPELLING to find the particular document required.

Other organisations might use different headings for clients or customers, for divisions of the company, for types of work, etc. For example, PRB510RR3W could be a document name indicating The Personnel Department (P), the author (RB), the document date (510 – 5 October), the nature of the document (RR – reference request) and document retention time (3W – 3 weeks). This type of coding is very useful where the index does not allow for lengthy document description, although it is not a very easy document name to remember. The essential point is that the naming of documents is controlled and therefore more likely to be efficient.

The acid test for any document is *can you find it?* Controlled naming helps. Another useful habit is to write the document name, and the disk on which it is to be found, on any draft of the document that is printed out. The DOCNAME could, if desired, be incorporated on the company's reference system on letters and other documents. On some systems it is automatically printed out at the bottom of each page.

**Indexing**    As has been said earlier, an index of what is on a disk will normally be compiled automatically by the machine, and you only have to give the commands to read the *index* to call to the screen exactly what each disk contains. A printout of the index can also be obtained.

There is sometimes a case for maintaining a manual index as well. Obviously the catalogue of document names, if this is maintained, serves as one type of index, but if the catalogue as described is not required, then a simple alphabetical index can be useful. Fig. 7.2 shows an example of a card index by client or customer name.

| Disk Name: | | | |
|---|---|---|---|
| Location: | | Client: | |
| DOCUMENT NAME | DATE | DESCRIPTION | NO OF PAGES |
| | | | |

**Fig. 7.2**

Here the name of the disk and where it is to be found can be details which can help locate a specific document quickly. The name of the disk would be the name to put on the disk label, and would be a general description of the content of the disk. The location would indicate where the disk is actually filed. A 'D' or 'C' after the disk name could also indicate that a duplicate or copy of that disk exists, and should be updated when any amendments to the documents on that disk are made.

In this case the *document name* is not allocated, but is created by the operator and the details on the card completed.

Fig. 7.3 shows an example of a partially completed index card kept, perhaps, by a firm of Builders and Decorators.

| Disk Name: *Office Renovation* | | | |
|---|---|---|---|
| Location: *E-H Container* | | Client: *J.F.W. Green* | |
| DOCUMENT NAME | DATE | DESCRIPTION | NO OF PAGES |
| *Greenest* | *29/06* | *Estimate for offices* | *4* |
| *Green sched* | *02/08* | *Agreed Schedule of Works* | *6* |
| *Addsched* | *17/09* | *Additions to Schedule* | *1* |

**Fig. 7.3**

It may seem a little cumbersome to maintain handwritten catalogues and indexes when the information and word processing equipment available is so sophisticated, and in the larger integrated systems, then this form of indexing is probably not required. However, if it helps people working in the organisation, of whatever size, to find what they want quickly, and with the minimum of fuss, then it is worth considering setting up and maintaining a manual indexing system.

**Filing** Disks must be filed away, and there are many containers available for storing disks of all sizes as described in Chapter 3. The important thing is that the containers should be of adequate size for the number and size of disks to be stored in them and should be convenient to store and handle. At least one storage area should be fireproof and if possible smoke proof, so that duplicate disks are not destroyed in the case of fire. This might mean having containers full of disks in an existing fireproof safe or cupboard, or it might mean buying purpose-built fireproof storage containers. Remember that smoke can badly corrupt disks, so that a totally different storage area for really vital information is advisable. This will naturally depend on the size and complexity of the system itself and the amount of work that is to be stored. Remember, too, that not only must work disks be safely stored, but back-up disks and secondary back-up disks need space and safe storage.

As with the labelling of the disks themselves, it is important that the storage locations are properly labelled so that a particular disk can be quickly located. Likewise the labels must show whether the disks stored are primary work disks or back-up disks. It is unwise to store back-up disks in exactly the same location as primary work disks, in case the disks in a particular storage area get lost or damaged. Keep them separate, but correctly labelled.

Floppy disks are sometimes stored in the boxes in which they are bought. This might be adequate for primary storage, but back-up disks should be kept in a more secure and fireproof location. There is a danger, too, that labels showing what the box contains are stuck on a removable lid, as shown in Fig. 7.4.

**Fig. 7.4**   Box with removable lid with label on lid

If disks are stored in the boxes in which they are bought, it is better to put the label on the box than on the lid, which can inadvertently be put on the wrong box. Fig. 7.5 shows a better way of labelling such a box.

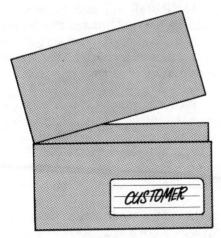

**Fig. 7.5**  Box with removable lid with label on box

These boxes, however, are not very satisfactory storage media, but can be useful for carrying disks around. There are, inevitably, special containers for transporting disks or sending them by post, and if a great deal of work is handled in this way, then these should be considered.

It is worth repeating on the subject of document naming, indexing and filing that the question which should always be asked is:

CAN YOU FIND IT?

If you *can* find it 100% of the time, then your procedures are working well.

**3  Disk care and management**
The care of disks is obviously important. Disks are not cheap in themselves, but above all they are the storage medium for long hours of work spent keying in and care in their use, handling and storage pays off.

As was mentioned in Chapter 3, there are disks of various types, sizes, densities and capacities. A good-quality floppy disk should last quite a long time, but one which is in constant use – the everyday software or system disk, for example – will probably eventually wear out. When this happens odd messages such as READ/WRITE

ERROR or SYSTEM ERROR will begin to appear on the screen, and this is the time to ask yourself whether the disk is worn out and needs replacement. Some manufacturers claim that their disks last a lifetime, and if this is so then well and good, but if things begin to go wrong on the system, it is as well to consider whether the fault could lie in the disk.

Hard disks are, of course, protected by plastic coverings. The main damage to them is from the 'heads' in the disk drive itself – the heads may become dirty if the atmosphere is full of dust or cigarette smoke, or they may crash down onto the disk if, for example, a drawer containing the disk is banged shut. If this happens the disk would be unusable and would need to be replaced – an expensive operation.

A disciplined method of working will enhance the life of a disk and decrease the possibility of losing valuable data.

Discipline, too, in which work goes on which floppy disk can make the operator's life easier, and lessen the cost of running the system. If a new disk is used every time a fresh document is to be created, then not only will the number of disks and back-up copies become unmanageable, but it will become an extremely costly operation. On the other hand a great diversity of work on one floppy disk can make documents difficult to find. A disciplined approach will make sure that a reasonable amount of related work is stored on any one disk. Thinking of a floppy disk as an old-fashioned paper file is a good way of deciding what shall go where.

Disks become full, of course, and then another must be used, and this happens to disks of all descriptions. It is advisable not to let any disk – floppy or otherwise – become too full before changing to the next one.

On a floppy disk, if you allow it to become more than, say 90% full, then there is no room to manouevre, and if you should want to do some complicated editing, then the capacity of the disk is insufficient to allow you to carry out the required tasks until some of the work has been deleted or moved to another disk. A full disk also means, of course, that there is no room for adding a page, or even a paragraph of work. The result can be odd bits of information or work having to be stored in spare places on other disks, which makes it difficult to find at a later stage.

It is as well to check the capacity remaining on disks before you use them and *as you go along* so that you will not find that you have one page left to key in and no disk space remaining.

Hard disks, too, inevitably get full, and as they do, so the response time (the time it takes between your giving a command and that command being executed) tends to get longer and the whole system slower. This can be very irritating when speed is of the essence.

Good disk care and management contributes much to the smooth running of any WP operation, and the same can be said of other WP stationery and materials.

### 4 Care and use of stationery and materials

In any organisation the organised and careful use of stationery and materials will bring economic benefits, and this is equally true of the word processing environment, particularly as its stationery and materials can be expensive.

When WP is first introduced into an organisation, people are often surprised to find that it engenders *more* paper rather than less. The main reasons for this seem to be:

(*a*) Slovenly drafting. Because writers of reports, etc. think that their written work can easily be amended, they tend to pay slightly less attention to their original drafts. The result is that where before three drafts were required, now perhaps there are four – more paper.

(*b*) Inadequate proof-reading. Many people find it more difficult to proof-read on the screen than from hard copy. Also, because mistakes can easily be corrected, accuracy in the original keying in can be less highly prized than if the whole document had to be re-typed. The consequence is that mistakes are corrected and another printout done – more paper.

(*c*) One of the beauties of WP is, as has been stressed earlier, the quality and appearance of the finished product. Operators strive, quite rightly, to make the final copy look good, and until they are used to the fact that what you see on the screen is not necessarily what comes out on the hard copy, they tend to experiment and to re-format – more paper.

(*d*) Hoppers and feeders usually require you to 'waste' several sheets to get the setting right on a long print run. If this is expensive headed paper, then the cost of wasted sheets, multiplied out, can be surprisingly high – more paper.

(*e*)   Unless operators are careful in the notes that they keep of printwheels and line spacing used on different documents, then paper – and time – is consumed on reprinting an amended document – more paper. This does not occur where large firms have standardised their printwheels and do not allow for individual tastes in print styles.

So the consumption of paper rises, at least for a while, rather than falls. At the same time, perhaps, expensive carbon ribbon is used and daisy wheels, if mishandled, can become misshapen. Labels are used for ordinary envelopes – because it is easier to print out labels than it is envelopes.

Naturally this seeming waste of materials has to be balanced against the increase in productivity resultant upon the introduction of WP. If real economies are sought, however, these are some of the ways in which they can be achieved in the use of stationery and materials:

(*a*)   When doing printouts and drafts which are to be amended, use fabric ribbons and scrap paper – or the back of old computer paper. You have to be careful that the paper you use does not contain confidential information. How many printouts of drafts are unnecessarily well-presented?

(*b*)   Make a note (on the draft or in the index) of the printwheel and print settings – margins, etc. – which were used. This will save time and paper on future printouts.

(*c*)   Take care of the consumables – the continuous stationery, the ribbons and printwheels, etc. There are storage facilities available for printwheels, if several of these are used, and they are well worth the investment of a small amount of money, particularly for plastic wheels.

(*d*)   It is possible to use carbons instead of the photocopier! Most printers will take up to two carbon copies satisfactorily. It does save on the photocopying in both paper and queuing time! Remember, too, that first-class hard copy provides a good master for offset litho printing, where this is applicable.

(*e*)   Regulate the number of printouts. It is, generally speaking, cheaper to print out a master copy on the WP and then photocopy, rather than doing several printouts. Of course, for a mail shot or documents where it is of the utmost importance that the original is used, this does not apply.

(*f*)  Use the computer, rather than paper, where it is possible. On large, integrated systems it should be possible to leave messages for people, to maintain records and carry out several other functions using the computer itself rather than paper. How many documents, records and pieces of information are stored on disk *and* hard copy?

WP consumables *are* expensive, and it is as well to remember that the efficient control and use of these can effect economies without prejudicing the speed or quality of the final product.

## 5  Workflow procedures

This is one of the office procedures which can properly grow out of experience of using the WP system and which, in an organisation of any size, needs to be disciplined and controlled. It is difficult to set up the correct procedures from the outset, but if an attempt is made, it is easier to alter the procedures in the light of experience than to try to sort out a muddle which has grown out of no procedures at all.

Naturally, the question of priorities for the work has to be tackled, but this is a normal management or supervisory function. Word processing imposes some additional constraints upon this management function, and these must be recognised if the communication between originator or author of the material and the operator is to be effective. This is an area where effective and efficient communication is most likely to break down, partly because a new WP installation does not know what it wants of its authors, and partly because the authors expect too much of the new WP installation.

When setting up a system of communication between author and operator, whether it is in a large company using pools or puddles of WP services, or whether it is a very small business with one operator, there are certain things the operator will need to know.

The main details required from an author are:

(*a*)  The nature of the document – whether it is a draft, top copy, for internal or external use, etc.

(*b*)  How many printouts and photocopies are required.

(*c*)   The choice of printwheels and line spacing, if discretion in these areas is allowed.

(*d*)   When the work is required. Authors must remember that initial keying in and printing out takes almost as long as typing.

(*e*)   How long the document is to be retained on disk. Some offices use a colour coding system for this routine.

(*f*)   Any special requirements, for example choice of paragraphs or clauses if document is to be boiler-plated, infills on a standard document, etc.

(*g*)   The confidentiality of the work. Keeping screenwork confidential and secure is not always so simple a matter as is the case with typewritten work.

Productivity on some systems can be measured by counting the number of keystrokes per hour, but speed of input is by no means the whole story. The real test of an efficient set-up is the turnround time of the work, which depends to a large extent on the management and control of the workflow. *How smooth is the workflow on your system?*

## 6   Security

The security of a system can literally mean how safe the various parts of the machinery are from theft. The more portable a machine becomes, the easier it is to walk out of the door with it, and if it is a popular make of machine, there will be no difficulty in buying the software to go with it.

The physical storage of disks containing confidential information is also an important aspect of security.

Floppy disks are easy to store in locked safes or other secure places. Hard disks, with a great deal of information on them which may be needed by several people, are harder to make physically secure – simply because of the size of the disk and the amount of information which has to be locked away.

If original disks are to be locked securely away because of the confidential information they contain, then backup disks must obviously be treated likewise, but kept in a different secure place.

Documents or disks containing confidential information can be protected by special security software so that only authorised people can access the document on the disk. This often takes the form of allocating a password to the document – the password has to be keyed in before the document can be called to the screen or printed out. In some cases the password itself is visible on the screen when it is keyed in, but in many security systems the password, or code of some description, is retained in the background – it does not appear on the screen. The only way of knowing whether the password, or code, is correct, and whether it has been correctly keyed in, is when the document or information required appears on the screen – or not! The list of codes or passwords itself then also needs to be kept secure.

Another security problem for confidential information is the actual keying in of the work itself. It appears on the screen for all to see, and is less easily concealed from the casual passer by than a piece of paper in a typewriter.

Specially designated terminals in a private environment is the answer here, together with strict routines for writing work away to the disk as soon as it is completed, and clearing the screen.

Because information stored on disk is so easy to amend, then there is the danger not only that unauthorised people can *read* confidential matters, but also that they can alter what they find.

So, from several points of view, security of information stored on disk can be a very important part of the WP installation.

Another aspect of security of information is whether documents can get lost or destroyed inadvertently or because of a breakdown of the system.

As has been mentioned earlier, documents can be 'protected' from accidental or malicious deletion, if the appropriate software is available and the correct protective commands given. An entire floppy disk can be protected from accidental erasure by taking the precaution of covering the slot on the edge of the disk with the protective 'label' provided (see Fig. 7.6).

The most effective way of ensuring that precious work is not accidentally lost when disks are corrupted by machine malfunction or some other cause, is to have sufficient backup copies. This is part of the 'housekeeping' routines which should be followed and which are explained in the next section.

Every place of work develops its own routines and 'office' procedures. Many of these routines are allowed to emerge rather than being planned and much time is lost through inefficiencies in this

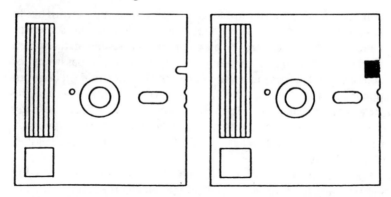

**Fig. 7.6**   Floppy disk with protective label affixed

area. It is not uncommon for people to blame the word processing system itself, or the operator, for lost work and lost time when it is in fact the office procedures which are at fault. It is an administrative and management matter which is often neglected when a word processing system is being installed, which is the very moment at which the opportunity to introduce efficient working practices should be seized.

## Housekeeping procedures

*Housekeeping* is the term normally used for the management and control of the machine and disks, as opposed to the office procedures which facilitate the running of the entire operation. Sometimes the word housekeeping is used to cover *all* procedures connected with making the system work.

### 1   Disk copying

This is a recurring theme. In Chapter 5 the *method* of disk copying was briefly described; in the previous section disk copying was mentioned under security. Here the subject of disk copying is treated yet again because it is so important.

Accidents do happen, systems do go down, disks do get corrupted, and unless you have a foolproof disk copying routine, then work can be irretrievably lost.

On some large mainframe systems the copying of data is automatically carried out, without the operator having to do anything special about it. For the most part, however, it is up to each operator to adhere strictly to the disk copying routines which must be set in train by the user.

Disk copying is a nuisance: it is time-consuming, and it is often done at the end of a working day or the end of a working session when the main thought is to close down the system. It is, however, *vital* to the maintenance of peace of mind and efficient word processing.

Some people may consider the time taken (several minutes per disk) and the cost of extra disks to be too expensive, but it is false economy to lose, for the sake of the price of a disk and the time it takes to copy it, perhaps a day's, perhaps a year's work. It has happened and it will happen again if disk copying is not done.

*System* or software disks should have not one but *two* copies. It is advisable, for one thing, to use a fairly fresh disk for initializing new work disks rather than an everyday system disk which might get rather worn. If a system disk gets corrupted then, quite simply, the machine will not work. A back-up disk can then be used to get the system going again. The second back-up disk then becomes the first back-up disk until a further back-up disk is created – one master and two copies are back in business. This is known as the *grandfather, father, son* system and is useful for many work disks as well as system disks. It works like this:

Suppose that on a Monday a certain amount of work is stored on a disk, and a copy is taken at the close of business – disk 1 is the father, disk 2 is the son. Father is stored in the fireproof safe, son is stored in a container ready for use the next day.

On the Tuesday, son (disk 2) is used and added to, and a copy is taken (disk 3). Disk 2 then becomes father and disk 3 becomes son. Disk 1 (in the safe) is therefore grandfather. The new father (disk 2) is stored in a second secure place and the new son (disk 3) is put in the container ready for the next day.

On the Wednesday the new son (disk 3) is used and added to, and a copy taken – not on a *new* disk, but on disk 1 (grandfather). Wednesday's son (disk 3) then becomes father; Wednesday's father (disk 2) becomes grandfather; and Wednesday's grandfather (disk 1) becomes Thursday's son.

Fig. 7.7 illustrates the sequence.

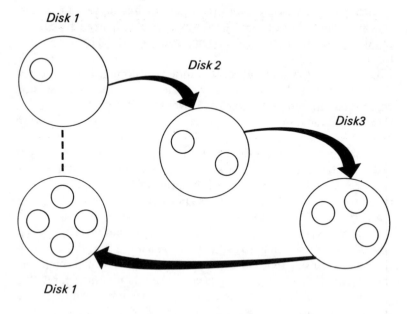

*Disk 1*

*Disk 2*

*Disk3*

*Disk 1*

**Fig. 7.7**   Grandfather, father, son disk copying

This copying procedure is used mostly on large systems where a considerable amount of data is added every day and where the copying process is somewhat lengthy. It means that at close of business only one copy need be taken instead of two, but there can never be more than one day's work lost. It also means that all disks are constantly updated.

It goes without saying that a record must be kept *with each disk* of when it is updated. On hard disks this can be a strip of paper fixed onto the plastic casing surrounding the disk recording the time and date of copying and the initials of the operator. Fig. 7.8 shows an example of a copying record which can be affixed to a hard disk.

For floppy disks a record is equally important, and can be written on the protective disk envelope, *provided that*

– the envelope has the name of the appropriate disk written on it, in case disks get in the wrong envelopes.
–any writing is done with the envelope empty of the disk.

# DISK COPYING RECORD

| DATE | TIME | OPERATOR |
|------|------|----------|
|      |      |          |
|      |      |          |
|      |      |          |
|      |      |          |
|      |      |          |
|      |      |          |
|      |      |          |

**Fig. 7.8** Disk copying record

It is possible to keep a separate record of disk copying in a book, but if the record is maintained on the disk cover itself, then there can be no possibility of muddling which disk is in question when a large number of different disks is in use.

The final word about disk copying is that everyone connected with the use of the word processing system must be made aware that disk copying is part of the normal, natural and *vital* routine, and that time must be set aside for it. If close of business is at 5.30 pm then authors should not expect work to be done at 5.15 pm. If they do, then the disk copying routine is disrupted and the copy may never be made – it might be that one disk that gets corrupted.

## 2 Controlling the disk space

Deletion of unwanted work has already been mentioned under the closing down procedure, so that daily control over the use of space is exercised.

There is also a need to control (at regular, say monthly, intervals) the amount of space taken up unnecessarily. It might be advisable to do this weekly where large amounts of data are concerned.

Inevitably there will be documents stored on disk which are no longer wanted. On the systems which, given the right commands, automatically delete documents after a certain length of time, there is no problem. Where this has to be done by the operator, then a regular time set aside for 'tidying up' the disks is a good method of trying to make sure that it is done. Here again, it is an irksome task to do, but it needs doing if disks full of unwanted work are not to accumulate.

When housekeeping the disks in this manner, it is as well to check with the originator of the material that deletion of the documents is in order. An operator cannot be expected to know for certain, unless systems of retention and deletion are very tightly controlled, whether documents will be needed again or not.

When documents are deleted, then the disk index will automatically be adjusted. Any manually maintained index will need updating, and this is where difficulties can arise if document names are allocated. When the document is deleted, do you re-allocate the name, or do you leave a gap in the sequence and take the next available name? In a sense it does not really matter which you do, as long as the procedure is followed by all.

The deletion of documents will leave spaces on the disk which can be filled by fresh documents. Because of the way in which the disk actually stores information, however, (as explained in Chapter 3) there do occur small gaps in the disk which can only be filled by *reclaiming the disk space*. Many systems have this facility, and where it exists it should be used. The appropriate commands must be given to reclaim the space, and the data on the disk is rearranged. Perhaps only an extra percentage point or two is made available, but it might make all the difference between having a disk almost and completely full.

### 3   Disasters

Disasters do occur. People who have worked with word processing for any length of time and not had a disaster of some sort can count themselves very fortunate.

Disasters come in all shapes and sizes. Some can be avoided, some cannot. The aim is to minimise disasters by preventive action or by quick cure. The former is, of course, preferable to the latter, but not always possible.

**Prevention** Newly designed systems tend to have teething troubles, so it is better, if possible, to buy in the first place hardware which has been tried and tested, and software in which the bugs have been found and removed. This sounds very basic and common sense, but new developments are exciting and tempting – they can, however, cause problems, especially to the small user who cannot command a high degree of back-up maintenance.

Regular maintenance is important. A maintenance agreement (for hardware and new software) can be arranged at the time of installation for all medium and large systems. What you get for your maintenance (the call-out time of the engineer, for example – is it 8 hours, 24 or longer?) will depend upon how much you are able to pay. You need to bear in mind that you become very dependent on your WP system, with work possibly locked into disks and totally inaccessible if the system does go down.

Maintenance agreements for small systems are less normal. Small systems do not often 'crash' or go wrong, particularly if a little preventive maintenance is carried out by the user (as opposed to the engineer). Kits are available for cleaning disk drive heads and these can be used regularly. Keeping strictly to the rules about no smoking, eating or drinking in the vicinity of the word processor also helps keep the system clean, as do the use of dust covers and the closing of disk drive doors.

Keeping the environment at a reasonable temperature will prevent fuses blowing because of the heat; keeping it free from pollution will prevent disk drive heads becoming dirty. While word processing systems do not need the carefully controlled environment of large computer systems, they *are* more sensitive than typewriters, and should be treated accordingly.

Loss of work of any kind is always a disaster, and this can best be prevented by following the rules about disk labelling, copying, correct disk handling and storage, etc.

Simply looking after the system as well as you are able will help to prevent disaster, whatever the size of the system.

**Cure**   If crashes do occur, or any other form of disaster, then they must be put right as quickly as possible. Remedies may range from 'Label the disk properly next time' to 'Call the engineer *immediately*'.

One of the great attributes of a good system manager is the ability to diagnose the fault and to know where and when to seek help.

Faults can be hardware, software or operator (liveware!) faults. Operator error is probably the most frequent cause of things going wrong, and this can happen through inexperience, lack of proper training, incompetence and many other factors. The system is frequently blamed for errors which are the fault of the operator, and good operators and system managers need to be aware of where the true cause of the breakdown lies.

Software faults are fairly rare, except when the program is new and not totally tested. There can be irritating quirks in the software – little things that the operator would prefer not to have to do – but these cannot be counted as software faults. An example of a software fault is when a correct command is given and the system does not carry out exactly what it has been asked to do – it does something slightly different, or does not do it at all. The only remedy if a genuine software fault is detected is to contact the supplier, who will turn to the programmer to put the matter right.

Hardware faults do certainly occur. The most likely faults are in the *printer* and the *disk drive*, because these contain some mechanical parts. Corrupt *disks* are also a major cause of breakdown, but the question is what has caused the disks to be corrupted – wear and tear, crashes of disk drive heads, incorrect handling and storage perhaps? The cause *could* be a hardware fault.

*Cables* can also be the cause of breakdowns. They can be found to be inadequate or wrongly installed if the system is added to in any way, or is asked to handle a different software program.

So, the fault can lie in one of several places, and the extent of the fault can vary considerably. Sometimes a system can crash completely – everything stops and the operator can do nothing at all with it. In such a case then the remedy is, without question, to call the engineer at once.

There can also occur minor faults that you can live with for a while, such as the printer failing to print a character occasionally. This is often the start of something more major, however, and should be carefully watched. Intermittent faults are usually the most difficult to diagnose and to cure.

All operators and system managers can help effect quick cures by maintaining a *computer fault book*. Engineers will always record what they have done to a machine, but they can be greatly assisted in their diagnosis if a very careful and accurate record is kept of everything that goes wrong with the system, however small. Fig. 7.9 shows the headings which can be used in a computer fault book.

# COMPUTER FAULT BOOK

| DATE | FAULT | DATE & TIME MONITORED | ACTION TAKEN |
|------|-------|-----------------------|--------------|
|      |       |                       |              |
|      |       |                       |              |
|      |       |                       |              |
|      |       |                       |              |
|      |       |                       |              |
|      |       |                       |              |

**Fig. 7.9** Computer fault book

Exact times and dates can be very important if a maintenance agreement is involved. The nature of the fault should be described as fully as possible, and the operator concerned should talk to the engineer, as useful pieces of information can sometimes be added verbally. The amount of downtime (the time when the system was out of action) should also be noted in case a history of malfunctions and time lost is needed.

The engineer is a very important link in the chain, and good working relationships should be cultivated. You feel utterly helpless when a crash occurs, and the more assistance and consideration you can give to the engineer, the quicker the fault – whatever it is – is likely to be cured.

Good system management undoubtedly comes with experience of word processing in general and of a specific system in particular. It will help, however, if you:

SET UP AND MAINTAIN

YOUR

OFFICE PROCEDURES

AND YOUR

HOUSEKEEPING PROCEDURES

MANAGE YOUR SYSTEM
DO NOT LET IT DICTATE TO YOU

# 8

# Words Processing Pitfalls

In gaining experience, several of the pitfalls of word processing will become all too painfully obvious. This chapter, however, is intended to point out the most likely pits into which the WP operator might fall, and the action which can be taken to prevent or remedy the situation.

## Losing work

The greatest amount of time wasted seems to be caused by losing work, either whole disks or separate documents or parts of documents. There are various reasons why work is lost, or cannot be found. There is a distinction here: work can be irretrievably lost, or it can be temporarily mislaid.

### 1   Total loss of work

| *Can be caused by:* | *Preventive action:* |
| --- | --- |
| Corrupt disks. | Have up-to-date back-up disks. Discard worn disks in time. Use correct disks for machine. Take care of disks. |
| Fire, smoke, water, etc. | Have up-to-date back-up disks in separate location if necessary. |
| System breakdown. | Regular maintenance and clean working environment. Have up-to-date back-up disks. |

| *Can be caused by:* | *Preventive action:* |
|---|---|
| Accidental deletion of whole disks or documents. | Have up-to-date back-up disks. Take care when deleting work. |
| Switching off machine while work is still on screen. | Follow the switching off/logging off procedure. Make sure other people know what *not* to do. |
| Failure to save or write work to disk (possible on some systems). | Remember *always* to write to disk or save the work at frequent intervals. On page-based systems write to disk *before* clearing the screen. |
| Re-writing or inserting the wrong page. | On page-based systems, check the screen page number is right *before* giving commands to re-write or insert. |

## 2 Temporary inability to find work

| *Can be caused by:* | *Preventive or remedial action:* |
|---|---|
| Looking for document on wrong disk. | Keep an up-to-date index or other recording system. |
| Inability to find correct disk. | Maintain a foolproof disk filing system. Label disks correctly. |
| Looking for document on disk in wrong disk drive. | Check 'read' commands given. You may have asked for work in the ∅ disk drive when it is in the 1 disk drive. |
| Document given unhelpful name. | Name documents in a sensible way – give full description. |
| Wrong document name keyed in. | Check 'read' commands given – it may be a simple keying in error. Check stops and spaces. |

| *Can be caused by:* | *Preventive or remedial action:* |
|---|---|
| Inability to relate hard copy to disk document (you have a printout of a document and cannot remember what you called it on disk). | Mark rough copy of printout with disk and document name. Maintain document index. |
| Inability to find specific paragraphs or pages in long documents, particularly when on several disks. | Mark rough copy with disk and page number. |
| Inability to find pages or sections subsequently added to a document. | Check that pages or sections were added to the correct document on the correct disk. Pages/sections can easily get added to the wrong document, particularly when several disks are being used. Leave sufficient space on disk for subsequent additions. |
| Inability to find work other people have done. | Ensure indexing system is followed by all concerned. |

## Keying in, editing and amending work

Many of the pitfalls under this heading are normal 'typewriting' hazards, such as inaccuracy, mis-spelling, inability to read handwriting, etc. There are, however, certain hazards peculiar to WP which, if known, can be avoided.

| *Keying in hazards:* | *Preventive or remedial action:* |
|---|---|
| Stops and spaces (e.g. REP2 for REP.2). | Check total accuracy, particularly when calling up documents or formatting work on screen. |
| '1' and '0' for numerics. | Always use 1 and 0, never 'l' and capital O. |

| *Keying in hazards:* | *Preventive or remedial action:* |
| --- | --- |
| Inconsistency in styles of heading, because the work has scrolled off the top of the screen, or is on previous screen pages. | On page-based systems, make rough printouts as you go. On document-based systems, scroll back to check, or make handwritten notes on heading styles. Use headers or buffer (temporary) memory. |
| Mis-placed carriage returns and tabs. | Check that all carriage returns and tabs are where they should be. They are often indicated on the screen. Give commands, if possible, to align the whole page or document before printing out. |
| Inaccurate emboldening or underlining. | Check that words or phrases to be emboldened or underlined are marked *at both ends*. On some systems it is easy to forget to do this or to delete the marking at one end accidentally. |
| Unusual symbols or characters are shown on keyboard but are not on printwheel – this particularly applies to fractions and accents and the £ sign. | Keep a printout of the characters found on each printwheel. Key in *all* keyboard characters, shifted and unshifted, and obtain printout. Check printwheel characters against keyboard characters. |
| Cursor will apparently not obey instructions to move up or down, left or right. | Check whether in edit or command mode. Check whether keys are shifted when they should not be. |

*Keying in hazards:*

*Preventive or remedial action:*

Cursor gets 'locked in'. It will not move, no matter what you do. Usually occurs when you have pressed the wrong function key.

Complete the sequence you have inadvertently started, and *then* give the commands to delete what you do not want. As a last resort, switch off and start again. You will probably lose the work on the screen.

Gobbledegook (rubbish) appears on screen. Usually occurs when impossible commands have been given. Nothing will move.

Normally switch off and start again. You will probably lose the work already on the screen.

Pressing wrong edit keys in haste deletes work you want to retain.

Check you have given right commands *before* pressing DELETE, ENTER, etc.

On long documents, calling up page from previous disks to use as format for new pages.

Give the same document name to the document on each disk. You then alter only the page number, not the document name as well, when calling the required page to the screen.

Forgetting which amendments have been made, because text has scrolled out of sight.

Tick off amendments on hard copy as they are done. Particularly valuable when interruptions are likely to occur.

Forgetting to give commands to re-write the document or page.

Check that amendments have been written to disk *before* clearing the screen.

Inconsistent line spacing when moving text.

Check line spacing is correct where text was before it was moved – there are often too many clear line spaces left. Check that line spacing is correct in new position to which text has been moved.

| *Keying in hazards:* | *Preventive or remedial action:* |
|---|---|
| Failure to delete unwanted text, particularly in cut and paste. | On some systems, once text has been moved from one page to another, the original remains where it is until specifically deleted. Check that this has been done. |
| Failure to correct each instance of an error particularly when formats, strings, etc., are saved and recalled. | Remember, when a particular sequence has been incorporated several times in a document, to amend *every* time an error appears. Use global search and replace. |
| Inconsistent page numbering, particularly after insertion or deletion of text. | If page numbering is done on screen, rather than automatically, remember to alter all page numbers as necessary. |
| Response to commands seems to be slow. | At start of business: *wait* for command to take effect. It is often slower the first time it is used after booting.<br>Later in the day: check that disk is not too full. |
| Failure to compensate for insertion or deletion of text. | If extra lines or line spaces are inserted at the top of a page, on page-based systems remember to compensate by deleting spaces or moving text at the bottom of the page. On screen-based systems remember to check the page break or use the repagination facility, if available. |

*Keying in hazards:*

*Preventive or remedial action:*

When using global search and replace, words requiring replacement are not found.

Check that word to be found is exact, for example 'train' will not be found if 'trian' is keyed in; 'customer' will not be found if 'Customer' (with a capital 'C') is keyed in.

In global search and replace, nonsense is made of sense of text.

Check that *every* instance of word found needs replacement, for example if 'centre' were to be replaced by 'middle' throughout the text, you would not wish to alter 'a sports centre' to 'a sports middle'. If in doubt, use *selective* search and replace (the system stops at each word found to allow you to amend it or not, as required).

## Printing out

*Printing hazards:*

*Preventive or remedial action:*

Changing printwheel pitch.

Remember to change print directives. A ten-pitch printwheel printed out in twelve-pitch spacing can look odd. Remember to alter the margin on the document. Ten pitch takes up more room on each line than twelve pitch, and considerably more than fifteen.
Remember to alter the page length if necessary, for the same reason.

Required character does not appear on printout.

Check character is on printwheel and in corresponding place on keyboard.

| *Printing hazards:* | *Preventive or remedial action:* |
|---|---|
| 'Device not ready', or equivalent, message appears on screen. | Check that printer is switched on, particularly when it has been switched off for changing wheels or ribbons. Check for loose cable connections. |
| Printer stops unexpectedly. | Check that ribbon has not run out. Indicator lights or screen messages may help you. Check that paper is loaded into printer or hopper, etc., and that there is sufficient ribbon. |
| Printer will not re-start. | Check that any 'Abort print' command has been cancelled. Check that casing on printer is correctly positioned – there is often a safety or 'trip' mechanism which will not allow the printer to print until all parts are correctly set. |
| Printout is faint or irregular. | Check that ribbon is correctly inserted and not worn out (if it is a fabric one). Check that plastic printwheels do not have bent petals. Check that printwheel is securely seated and fixed. |
| Gobbledegook is printed out. | Check that printwheel is compatible with printer and software. |
| Printing operation does not 'sound' right. | Check the following: <br><br>–Printer could be out of paper at bottom of page and printing direct on to platten. |

*Printing hazards:*

*Preventive or remedial action:*

–Paper could be crumpled up under bail bar.

–Paper (and particularly labels) could have wrapped themselves round platten.

–Continuous stationery could have come off the sprockets on the tractor feed.

–Thick paper or envelopes may not be turning up properly.

Printout does not appear in correct position on paper.

Check the following:

–Top, bottom, left and right margins are correct, particularly if printwheel has been changed *or* margins have been previously altered (e.g. for printing out an envelope) *or* a hopper or tractor feed is used.

–Spacing directives are correct – double spacing changed to single will alter layout of page or document.

–Paper is inserted in printer at correct position. The possible reasons for incorrect positioning are:

–Imprecise paper guide on printer.

–Printer automatically turns up paper a little before it starts printing.

–Hoppers and tractor feeders can move paper up less than accurately. The problem gets worse as the print run continues.

| *Printing hazards:* | *Preventive or remedial action:* |
|---|---|

Page breaks are incorrect, resulting in widows and orphans, breaking in middle of paragraphs, incorrect page numbering, etc.

If printing continuously, check pagination directives. If printing page by page, check that number of lines is correct for the length of the page. For example, if you have been printing out labels with a page length of 09 and then print an A4 sheet without first altering the page length, the printer will stop after line 9.

Columns in tabulated work are out of alignment.

Check that the correct number of tabs and carriage returns have been inserted in the document, and that text has not wrapped itself round through lack of space.

In double-column work where text and side headings are used, headings sometimes do not appear on same line as first line of appropriate text, for example:

Adjust position of heading in right-hand column by inserting or deleting clear line spaces. The heading will appear incorrect on the screen, but correct on the printout.

| TEXT | HEADING |
|---|---|

Managers are responsible for ensuring that all employees keep strictly to time . . .

TIME
KEEPING

| *Printing hazards:* | *Preventive or remedial action:* |
|---|---|
| Underlining or emboldening is incorrect. | Check directive given in document. <br> *Note:* In double-column work, the underlining on the screen will sometimes seem to go across both columns where underlining was only required in the left hand column. The printout will be correct. |
| Dashes or brackets which should be underneath each other appear out of alignment, for example: | Use a tab setting where you want the brackets to be. |

```
In witness whereof   )
I have hereunto        )
set my hand this     )
     day of        )
```

(This often happens with proportional printwheels.)

Word processing can be extremely frustrating, especially for beginners. As you can see, there are many little things which can go wrong and which require amendments and re-prints – these can be almost as time-consuming as losing the work altogether. Attention to detail at the keying in stage and, above all, at the printing out stage can obviate many of the minor catastrophes. Major disasters can often be avoided, too, by careful system management.

# 9

# WP Knowledge, Skills and Aptitudes

Much of the knowledge and skill required by the competent WP operator will be learned through good training followed by experience. There are certain areas of knowledge and skill and certain aptitudes which pre-dispose a potential WP operator to become a competent one. Large companies are able to use various tests to ascertain whether potential operators will become competent, but small companies and individuals can only rely on general guidelines to help them assess a person's abilities and possible future competence.

It is not true to say that word processing is so easy that 'any fool can do it'. Word processing does not happen 'at the press of a button', and operators need to possess certain aptitudes and skills in addition to receiving sound training.

## Knowledge

Before embarking on word processing, the knowledge required is very much related to general 'typewriting' work in particular, and office work in general. It is certainly useful to know how to follow set procedures, to know the accepted conventions for layout of various documents, to be familiar with general office routines of indexing, filing, etc., and to know how the various office machines can be used to the best advantage. It is *not* necessary to have a thorough working knowledge of computers, nor, to start with, even a basic knowledge of hardware, software and computer terminology. The basics can be learned – and should be learned as allied knowledge – as the new operator masters the machine skills necessary to become competent.

## Skills

### 1 Machine skills

Fluent keyboard skills, preferably with touch typing, are essential to good WP operation. Word processing, unlike data processing, requires considerable input of text, so that accurate alpha keyboarding is of paramount importance.

Accuracy is more valuable than speed, in spite of the fact that errors are easy to correct. Corrections break the flow of the work and are time-consuming.

The use of the various function and edit keys will be learnt during the training period, but a potential operator will become proficient that much more quickly with good keyboarding skills.

### 2 English language skills

Also essential is a sound knowledge of and ability to use the English language, and this covers spelling, grammar and punctuation. A word processing machine will *not* enable a poor user of English to improve – machines do not construct sentences and insert punctuation without the correct input from the operator. They can *check* spelling and are very useful for inputting highly technical terms, but a good operator should have the ability to spell, with 100% accuracy, vocabulary that is commonly and regularly used.

### 3 Proof-reading skills

Proof-reading skills are obviously very much allied to English language skills – without the latter it is difficult to detect that an error has been made, in many instances. Proof-reading skills also cover the ability to spot keying errors and inconsistencies in heading styles, paragraph and page numbering, etc.

A new operator may well find it more difficult to proof-read from screen than from hard copy, but it is a distinct advantage to have sound proof-reading skills generally. Not only will you need to detect errors in the text, you will also need to be able to interpret screen messages and markings, and to spot when, for example, a tab mark or carriage return is missing.

**4 Layout skills**

A knowledge of the conventions for the layout of documents is highly desirable, as has already been said. The skills required to put this knowledge into practice are equally desirable. You still, when using a word processor, need to be able to work out heading styles, tab positions, page layout, margins, etc. Indeed, layout skills, and the ability to envisage what the appearance of the work will finally be, is even more important than on a typewriter.

The reasons for this are that, first, people *expect* work done on the word processor to look immaculate, and second, what comes out on the printout is not necessarily what you see on the screen. A good level of layout skill, while not essential, is highly desirable.

# Aptitudes

While certain skills are essential to a potential operator before starting word processing, and a general knowledge of office work, layout, etc., is useful, the personal attributes and aptitudes that a potential operator possesses – or does not possess – will go a long way to determining how competent that operator will become.

Desirable attributes, not in order of merit, are:

### A disciplined approach

It is necessary to work in a very disciplined manner, and to work tidily. Routines and procedures must be followed, records maintained and working areas kept tidy, or work will be lost. It takes a lot of self-discipline to carry out the copying and housekeeping procedures, for example, which in themselves seem unproductive and yet which are necessary to the smooth working of the system.

### Logic

As we have seen, the word processor will do only what it is told to do, and must be given precise, logical instructions. Logic is needed, too, for solving problems – it is fairly easy to remember what you have done one step back if something goes wrong, but more difficult to retrace your steps further back unless you have a logical sort of mind.

**A good memory**
This is not essential, but can be very helpful in remembering sequences, commands, codes, etc.

**Concentration**
Word processing is very concentrated work, and good powers of concentration in areas where there are several other things happening are a great asset. You need to be able to concentrate totally on the work in hand to get it right first time.

**Patience and perseverance**
If the work does not go right, then you need great patience to get it 100% accurate, particularly when you have already done several printouts and it *still* does not look right. Perseverance comes in as well, and the determination not to give up before the final product is of the highest quality.

**Standards**
High standards of accuracy and presentation are essential, otherwise the value of the word processor is, to a large degree, lost.

**Flexibility and adaptability**
Things often go wrong, or change in some way – the software could be updated, for example, or the system could go down just when it is most urgently needed. Flexibility, adaptability and calmness are needed in these situations. You are so dependent upon the machine that you feel quite helpless until it is up and running again – panic during a breakdown can lead you to try inadvisable things (copying from corrupt disks, for example) and a flexible, philosophical approach is needed.

**Ability to follow instructions accurately**
Not only must you be able to follow the routines and procedures laid down, you must also be able to read and interpret training and user manuals. If you do not follow the instructions absolutely accurately, then the system simply will not work.

**Creativity**
At the same time you need to be able to use your intelligence and

your inspiration to use the word processor in an interesting way, and be prepared to try innovative sequences to find the best solution to a presentation problem, for example. You must be able, too, to present work which can be used creatively on the photocopier to enhance its appearance.

### Machine empathy
It is helpful if you are happy working with machines and do not mind experimenting with them or diagnosing faults when they go wrong.

### Administrative ability
You will often need to set routines or sequences yourself, for future ease of working, and of course your administrative ability will come into play in all aspects of system management.

### Working with other people
Although you are working with a machine, the ability to communicate and get on with people is essential. You are often providing a service for other people, unless your word processor is for your own personal, private use. There will be deadlines to meet and explanations to be given, instructions to be received and understood and problems to be solved in conjunction with other people. Although word processing requires high levels of concentration, it is not a job to be done in isolation.

Who, then, should learn or teach themselves word processing? The answer is anybody with the basic knowledge and skills and at least some of the aptitudes mentioned above.

It is thought by some that older people will find it difficult to master a word processor – experience has shown that the age of a person is, in the end, immaterial. Younger people seem to learn how to work the machine quite quickly, but sometimes lack the English language and display skills of older people. Older people can take longer to learn and remember the commands, disciplines and sequences required, but once they *have* learnt what they need to know, they can bring their maturity, logic, work experience and other attributes to bear, and will often make excellent operators.

Some people, perhaps, will never learn how to do word processing, however hard they try, but then again, some people will never learn how to master a keyboard of any sort.

Word processing need not be an occupation reserved for an elite few, nor, on the other hand, is it necessarily open to all and sundry, because of the skills and aptitudes required to make it work. It is taking its place naturally in the world of office automation, both at the place of business and in the home. It takes a lot of the drudgery out of the processing of words, but imposes its own requirements of logic, discipline, creativity and high standards of accuracy and presentation.

Above all, the word processor enables you to produce quickly and efficiently work which is totally accurate and aesthetically pleasing. It is a skill and an art well worth learning.

# Glossary of WP Terms

**Abbreviation file**  The facility to give abbreviations to often-repeated words and phrases, so that when the abbreviation is keyed in, the whole word or phrase will appear.

**ABORT**  Means stop.

**Acoustic hood**  A 'hood', usually made of plastic, which goes over the printer to cut down the noise.

**Alpha/numeric sort**  The facility to sort lists, etc., alphabetically or numerically, ascending or descending.

**Amend**  To make corrections and alterations to a text already keyed in.

**Anti-static**  A spray, mat or other medium which will reduce the static electricity in the atmosphere.

**ASCII**  The American Standard Code for Information Interchange. It is a well-known machine code.

**Automatic page numbering**  A facility which allows you to give commands to number pages automatically, according to your needs.

**Background**  Processes go on 'in the background' while you are using the screen for something else. For example, one document can be 'background' printed while you are keying in another document.

**Back-up**  Systematic copying and secure storage of information on copy disks. The second copy is often called a *Security Disk*.

**BASIC**  A computer language. Stands for Beginners All-purpose Symbolic Instruction Code.

**Binary**  The code in which computers work, consisting of combinations of 0's and 1's.

**Bit**   Each coded 0 or 1 in the binary system.

**Block move**   The function of moving a block of text from one part of a document to another. Also known as *cut and paste*.

**Boiler-plating**   Merging pre-stored documents or paragraphs together to make one required document.

**Boot**   To 'boot' is to set the system going – pull it up by its boot straps.

**Buffer**   Temporary memory where data is stored before processing.

**Bug**   A program error.

**Byte**   Short for 'by eight'. 8 bits = 1 byte.

**Carbon ribbons**   High quality ribbons which can be used only once.

**Cartridge disks**   'Hard' disks encased in plastic with a large memory capacity.

**Centring**   The ability to centre text between the margins.

**Character**   Any letter, figures, symbol or space which can be displayed.

**COBOL**   Common Business Orientated Language – a computer language.

**Column manipulation**   The facility to move tabulated columns around the screen.

**Command driven**   The software is controlled by special command words keyed in by the user.

**Commands**   Messages keyed in to command the computer to execute the required function.

**Command strings**   Strings of words, phrases, etc. that can be called to the screen by giving the correct commands.

**Configuration**   The whole hardware set-up of the system – terminals, CPUs and peripherals.

**Continuous stationery**   Stationery which can be fed through the printer continuously, like traditional computer paper.

**CPU**   Central Processing Unit – the central control unit of any computer.

**CRT**   Cathode Ray Tube. Sometimes used to mean the screen.

**Cursor**   The (often) flashing square, oblong or line which tells you where you are on the screen.

**Cut and leave**   The function of putting text into temporary memory and using it in another part of the document, while leaving the original where it is.

**Cut and paste**   The function of moving text from one part of the document and 'pasting' it in to another. Also known as *block move*.

**Daisy wheel**   The print head made of plastic or metal which looks like a daisy, with a character on each petal.

**Daisy wheel printers**   Printers which use daisy wheels and which produce high-quality printout.

**Data**   Any information, figures and words which are to be processed into meaningful material.

**Dedicated WP**   A system 'dedicated' almost entirely to word (not data) processing.

**Default**   The values (for margins, pitch, etc.) pre-set in the software. The system will 'default to' the pre-set value unless instructed otherwise.

**Device**   The various parts of the configuration. Can be a printer or a disk drive or a screen. 'Device not ready' probably means something is not switched on.

**Diagnostic**   Used to find faults – often refers to disks which an engineer uses.

**Disk**   The storage media used by many computers – hard, floppy and Winchester are examples.

**Disk drive**   The part of the computer which 'reads' the information on the disks. This is where the disks are inserted.

**Document assembly**   The process of creating named or numbered paragraphs which can be stored and then called to the screen by keying in the appropriate name or number.

**Dot matrix printer**   The printer has a battery of pins which create characters from a pattern of dots.

**Double columns**   Two columns of work, each of which is an entity and can be amended, justified, etc., without affecting work in the other column.

**Electronic mail**   A service which allows computer terminals to dial up over the telephone network to consult personal electronic mailboxes. Used for sending messages between computers.

**Embolden** To embolden is to command the printer to overprint two to four times so that the print appears in bold type.

**Enhance** To enhance a system is to buy further, normally more powerful, devices or software to add on to the existing system.

**EXIT** A command often used to get out of a program.


**Fabric ribbons** Ribbons made of nylon fabric for use in daisy wheel printers. Can be used until too faint.

**Field** A specific area on the screen or in a document – on a form you have a 'field' for the name, address, etc.

**File** A named 'document' created and held in the computer's memory.

**Floppy disk** A round disk in a square protective casing which is flexible – hence floppy. Comes in various sizes (3½", 5¼", 8").

**Floppy disk drive** A drive in which you insert floppy disks.

**Footers** Page numbers and other information, such as footnotes, found at the bottom of a page.

**Font** The typeface or printstyle. Each printer can use several different fonts, depending on the power of the software.

**Format** To format – to prepare or initialize a disk. A format – the way a document is set up (margins, tabs, etc.).

**FORTRAN** A computer language particularly used by mathematicians (from FORmula TRANslator).

**Function keys** Keys additional to the normal alpha-numerical keys on the keyboard which allow you to perform specific WP functions.


**GIGO** A commonly used equation: Garbage In = Garbage Out – in other words if you input rubbish, then rubbish will be produced and printed out.

**Global search and replace** The facility to search out, automatically, throughout a document, a word or phrase and replace it with another.

**GO** A command often used to set a system going.


**Hard copy** Printout (on paper).

**Hard disk** A large round disk encased in plastic. Also called a *cartridge disk*. Has large memory capacity.

**Hardware** The mechanical, electronic and plastic pieces of a computer. If you can touch it, it's hardware.

**Headers** Headings, page numbers and other information found at the top of each page.

**HELP** A facility on many systems which helps you to diagnose where you have gone wrong and put matters right.

**Highlight** To 'highlight' a word, sentence, etc. on the screen means to define/delineate the word, sentence, etc. with which you wish to deal.

**Hot zone** The region at the end of each line so many characters in from the right-hand margin. The zone can be set by the operator. Words within this zone require hyphenation, or will be wrapped round.

**Index** The catalogue or list of documents/files stored on a disk.

**Initialize** To 'prepare' a blank disk for use on a specific system.

**Input/output (I/O)** Input is the information fed into the computer. Output is the information produced by the computer.

**Interface** A specially-constructed box and/or cable which allows different parts of the computer to communicate with each other.

**Justification** The right-hand margin, like the left, is 'justified' so that it is printed out with a straight right-hand margin. The characters are spaced out to fill up the line, as in true printing.

**K** Literally, a thousand. There are 1024 bytes in a Kilobyte (K). Used to express the amount of memory available on a system – for example 32K, 64K, etc.

**Language** Writing programs in binary, which the computer understands, is too difficult and cumbersome. Therefore languages (e.g. BASIC, COBOL, FORTRAN), which are more like English, allow programmers to write more easily. Programs are written in these languages and then translated (by the computer) into binary or 'machine' code.

**List processing** The facility to merge, for example, names and addresses with a 'form' or standard letter and print out. Often called *mail merge*.

**LOGON/LOGOFF**  A phrase often used on mainframe computers, and WP packages attached to them, asking you to 'log on' – in other words enter the program. Similarly used to exit from the program.

**Mail merge**  The facility to merge, for example, names and addresses with a 'form' or standard letter. The letter only has to be keyed in once. The merge and printing takes place automatically. Sometimes called *list processing*.

**Mainframe**  A powerful computer of large capacity and versatility, usually used by large organisations.

**Maths pack**  A program which allows the operator to do simple mathematical calculations on the computer.

**Memory**  A measure of the power of the computer is its memory capacity. 132K means that the computer has the capacity for 132 thousand bytes of memory.

**Menu**  Alternatives presented to the user on the screen so that the required function can be selected. Menu-based systems are normally easier to use than command-based systems.

**Micro**  The smallest of the computers. Can usually do word and data processing, but not simultaneously.

**Mini**  A smaller version of a mainframe computer. Can usually do word and data processing simultaneously.

**Modem**  Short for modulator/demodulator. It enables you to attach your computer to a telephone line, translating computer signals into those used by the telephone network.

**Moderate**  Means to alter (text). You can re-call a document to the screen, moderate it, and file it away again in the computer's memory – or print it out.

**Mouse**  A free-moving device which moves the cursor on the screen to required positions.

**Move**  The facility to move text around the screen.

**Multi-strike**  High-quality carbon ribbons.

**Numeric pad**  The layout of numeric keys usually on a pad to the right of the main keyboard. Sometimes incorporated in the main keyboard.

**Operating system**   The 'heart' of the software. It ensures the correct interpretation of commands, etc.

**Operator disk**   The disk on which the main word processing (or other) software program is stored to make the system work. Often called the *system disk*.

**Optical character reader (OCR)**   A machine which can 'read' typescript directly into a word processor. Can usually only read specified fonts.

**Pagination**   The facility to break a long document into given page lengths (usually between 55 and 60 lines to an A4 page).

**Peripherals**   The printers, disk drives, keyboards, etc. which enable information and programs to be fed in and out of a computer.

**Print setting**   The margins (top, bottom, left and right) and page length set for a page of printout.

**Printwheel**   Another name for a daisy wheel.

**Program**   The instructions written to make the machine obey certain commands, etc. Note the spelling.

**QWERTY**   The name given to the familiar typewriter keyboard – from the first six letters on the top line of alpha keys.

**RAM**   Random Access Memory.

**Read/write commands**   Commands given to the word processor to 'read' a document or 'write' it to disk.

**ROM**   Read Only Memory.

**SAVE**   To 'file' the work created on the screen on disk, or other storage medium, or in a temporary memory.

**Scratch file**   A facility for putting text into temporary memory.

**Scrolling**   The action of moving the text up and down the screen, and to left and right.

**Search and replace**   The facility to find a word or phrase throughout a document so that the operator can replace it with another word or phrase. Often called *selective search and replace* (see also *global search and replace*).

**Security disk**   A second back-up copy of a disk.

**Shared logic**   A hardware system where several terminals share the CPU, software and printers.

**Single sheet feeder** A device attached to the printer which will automatically feed in single sheets of paper.

**Software** Refers to all programs run on computer hardware – the instructions which make the machine work.

**Split screen** The facility to call up parts of two pages on the screen at the same time. The screen is split to allow for this.

**Standalone** A small hardware system which is complete in itself, comprising VDU, CPU, disk drives, keyboard and printer.

**Status line** The line, usually at the extreme top or bottom of a screen, which shows the 'status' of the work – line number, character number, etc.

**Storage disk** The disk on which is stored the work you have created. Sometimes called a *work disk*.

**SYNTAX ERROR** A phrase used to tell you that you have keyed in something incorrectly.

**System disk** The disk on which the main word processing (or other) program is stored to make the 'system' work. You cannot boot the system up without it. Sometimes called a *software* or an *operator disk*.

**Terminal** The screen and keyboard together make a terminal.

**Thimble** A type of print 'wheel' shaped like a thimble.

**Tractor feeder** An accessory which clips on top of the printer to ensure that continuous stationery goes in straight.

**Turnkey** A system installed for you, normally by a consultant, which is 'up and running' and ready to go. You only have to 'turn the key'.

**Unbundle** Systems are often sold as a total package – hardware, software, training, etc. To 'unbundle' is to sell each part separately.

**User friendly** This means that the system should be easy to use and that the messages on the screen are clear and comprehensible, and not written in computer jargon.

**VDU** Visual Display Unit – the screen.

**Wide screen** A facility which allows you to extend the right-hand margin beyond the normal 80. The screen itself remains the same size.

**Widows and orphans**   These occur when printing out long documents. The page number, etc., appears at the top of the next page (the orphan) instead of the bottom of the correct page (the widow).

**Winchester Disk**   A small compact hard disk unit often found with micros.

**Work disk**   The disk (of whatever type) on which you store the work you have created. Also called a *storage disk*.

**Workstation**   The place where an operator sits and works – includes desk, chair, terminal, etc.

**Wraparound**   The facility which automatically transfers a word that is too long for the line onto the next line. No need to use the RETURN key.

# Index

*Note: numbers in italics refer to illustrations.*

abbreviation files/strings, 37
abort, 42, 96
accessories, 70–8
acoustic hoods, 74, *75*, 89
alignment, 34–5, 190, 191
amendments, 17, 26–7, *28*, 40, 183–7
   assignments, 111, 116, 129, 131, 138
   *see also* updating
anti-static spray/mats, 78, 86
applications software, 59, 60
aptitudes for word processing, 194–7
ASCII, 58
atmosphere, 86–7
auto tab *see* inset text
automatic
   deletion, 41
   duplication, 41–2
   page numbering, 43–4, 138

back-up, 164, 171
background, 198
   merging, 37
   printing, 45, 138
backing store, 48
BASIC, 58
binary, 58
bit, 58
block
   copy, 34
   move, 34
boiler plating, 24, 25, 38
booting, 91
buffer, 38, 135
bulk mailing, 17–23
byte, 58, 59

cables, 48, 55, 178
cartridge disks *see* hard disks
cassette tape, 64, *65*
catalogue, 40, 41
centring, 35, 114, 131, 135
characters, 31, 34, 50, 58
closing down, 116–20
COBOL, 58
code-based systems, 105
column manipulation, 31, 38, 190
command-based systems, 105
commands, 96, 98–9, 115–16
communications, developments in,
   2–4, 11, 14
compatibility, 63–4
computer
   fault book, 179
   languages, 57–8
configurations, 55, *57*, 60–3
continuous
   printing, 44
   stationery, 72, 79, *80*, *81*
correcting text, 34, 109–11, 186
corrupt disks, 178, 181
CP/M system, 58, 63
CPU (central processing unit), 47, 48,
   55, 59, 61
CRT (cathode ray tube), 50
cursor, 34, 106, 184–5
   control keys, 106–8, *106*, *107*,
   110
cut
   and leave, 34
   and paste, 34
   sheet paper, 78

daisy wheel, 52, *53*, 70–1
 printer, 52, 54
data processing, 5–7, *6*, 14
de-skilling, 8–9, 11
decor, 87
dedicated
 keys, 107, *107*
 word processors, 61–2
default, 108
delete, 96, 110, 111, 114, 117–18, 185
 automatic, 41
density of disk, 65
disasters, minimisation of, 176–80
disk drives, 55, *56*, 61
diskettes, 55, 64–8
disks
 care of, 67–8, 165–7
 cartridge *see* disks, hard
 copying, 118–19, 172–5, *174*, *175*
 deletion of data, 67
 floppy, 55, 64–8, *65*, *66*, 91
 formatting, 63, 92
 hard, 55, 64, *65*, *66*, 68–9, *68*
 initialisation, 63, 64, 92
 labelling, *92*, 93
 loading, 91
 management, 27, 29, 165–7
 protection, 171, *172*
 space, 40, 41, 166–7, 175–6
 storage, 74, *77*, 125, 163, 164–5, 170
 Winchester, 68
document
 compilation, 17, 24–6
 copying, 118–19
 creation, 100–2
 deletion, 117–18, 176
 description, 101–2
 naming, 27, 40, 100–2, 160–1, *161*,
  182
document-based systems, 102, 104,
 162–3
DOS system, 58, 63
dot matrix printer, 52, *53*
double columns, 38, 153, 190
drafting, 17, 26–9, *28*, 167
dual-sided disk, 65
duplication, automatic, 41–2
dust, effect on disk, 86

edit, 98–9, 183–7
electronic
 diary, 13–14
 mail, 12–13
 messaging, 12–13
emboldening, 44–5, 114, 122, 131, 191
ENTER key, 96, 108, 116
envelopes, 131
error messages, 55, 97–8
EXECUTE key, 116
eye-strain, from VDU, 88

faults, 178–9
FAX (facsimile transmissions of
 documents), 11–12, *12*
feeders, 72–4, *73*
fields, 32
figures, 31–2, 93
files, 100–2
filing, 160, 163–5
fire precautions, 163
floppy disks, 55, 64–8, *65*, *66*, 91
flush right facility, 135
font, 42, 70, 71
footers, 44, 138
form letters, 17, *18*, *19*, 37, 146
formats, 129, 131
formatting disks, 63, 92
forms, 32–3, *33*, 38
FORTRAN, 58
function keys, 48, 49, *49*
furniture, 83–5

glare on screen, 52, 85, 87
global search and replace, 37, 138, 187
grandfather, father, son system, 173–4,
 *174*
graphics, 7–8, *8*, 14, 38

hard
 copy, 27, 29
 disks, 55, 64, *65*, *66*, 68–9, *68*
  care of, 166
 space, 111
hardware, 47–57
headed paper, 131
headers, 44
HELP! facility, 38–9
highlighting of text, 114
horizontal
 lines, 44
 scrolling, 149
hot zone, 35
housekeeping procedures, 157, 158,
 172–80

hyphenation, 35

indented paragraphs, 131
index, 40, 41, 162
indexing, 160, 161–3, *162*, *163*
information processing, 7–8, 14
initialising disks, 63, 64, 92
ink jet printer, 52
input, 4, 17, 34–40
   devices, 48–50
input/output (I/O), 55
insert, 32, 96, 110, 114, 182, 187
insertion documents, 24, 25
inset text, 36, *36*, 131
interface, 63
interpreter, 58
interrupt print, 42
I/O, 55

justification (right-hand), 43, 122, 138

K, 48, 59
keyboard, 7, 14, 48–9, *49*
keying in, 29, 44, 93–4, 106–9, 111, 122
   errors, 59
   hazards, 183–7
keys, 49
kilobyte, 59
knowledge required for word
     processing, 192–3

labels, 79, *81*, 131
landscape work, 36, 149
laser beam printers, 52
layout skills, 135, 194
lighting, 85
line spacing, 43, 108, 138, 185
   deletion,111
   insertion, 110
list processing, 17, 146
loading software, 91, 93
log on/off, 60, 91, 92, 119–20, 158–60,
    182
losing work, 181–3
lower case, 36, 114

machine codes, 57–8
magnetic tape, 64, *65*
mail
   merge, 17, 20–1, *22*, *23*, *24*, 37, 146
   shot, 46, 79
mainframe, 60–1, 64

maintenance, 177
manipulation of text, 3, 4, 113–15
margins, 35, 108, 111, 122, 125, 131
master copy, 44
maths pack (mode), 31, 38
memory, 3, 16, 47–8, 59
menu-based systems, 104–5
menus, 91, 104
micro, 60, 61
mini, 60, 61
modem, 13
modifying text, 116
mouse, 108
moving text, 34, 114, 138
multiple copies, 17, 44

networks, 62–3
numerics, 31–2, 93–4

OCR machines (optical character
    readers), 48
office procedures, 157, 158, 172
opening a file, 100–2
operating system, 58–9
output, 4
   devices, 50–5, 56

page-based systems, 103–4
page
   breaks, 102, 190
   numbering, 43–4, 138
pagination, 43
paragraphing, 43, 111
password, 42, 171
peripherals, 48–57
personal computers, 62
personalised letters, 21, 23
photocopiers, 9
pollution, effect on word processors,
    86–7
power supply, 86
print
   abort, 42, 188
   head, 52, 70
   interrupt, 42
   pitches, 42, 71, 108, 138, 187
   queues, 45–6
   selections, 46
   settings, 97
   stands, 74, *77*
   styles, 42, 70–1
   wheels, 45, 52, *53*, 70–1, *70*, 184

printers, 52–4, 188
printing
    continuous, 44
    hazards in, 187–91
    from screen, 45
    single, 44
    white on black, 45
printing out, 29, 42–6, 116, 122, 131
    *see also* printing hazards
printout, 17, 19, 52
    catchers for, 74, *76*
    faint, 188
    trolleys for, 74, *76*
program, 57
proofreading, 167, 193
protected field, 32, *33*, 111

QWERTY, 48

RAM (random access memory), 48, 59,
    60
re-writing, 116, 182
read commands, 116
recall from disk, 116, 129, 131
reclaim disk space, 41, 67, 177
retrieval, 14, 17, 40
RETURN key, 96, 108, 116
reversible disk, 65
ribbons, 72, *72*
rigid disks *see* hard disks
ROM (read only memory), 58

safety, 88–9
saving text, 115, 129, 182
scratch files, 38–9, 135
screen, 36, 39, 49–52, *50*, *51*, 94–5
    messages, 55, 94–8
scrolling, 36, 149
search and replace, 36–7, 138, 187
security, 41, 42, 170–2, *172*
shared logic system, 61–2
single
    printing, 44
    sheet feeders, 72–3, *73*
single-sided disk, 65
skills of operator, 8–9, 11, 193–4
smoke, effect on disks, 86, 163
software, 16, 33–4, 57–60, 62
sorting, 39
spelling package, 38
split screen, 38
standalone system, 62

standard letters, 20, 21
stationery, 78–82, 167–9
status line, 95
storage, 14, 17, 40–4, 47–8, 115
    disk, 91
    media, 64–9
    temporary, 38, 47–8, 135, 149
switching on/off, 51, 52, 158–60, 182
syntax error, 59
system disk, 91, 173
system specification, 48

tabs, 35, 125, 131, 149
tabulation of figures, 31, *31*, 32, *32*,
    38–9
telex, 13
temperature, 86
temporary storage, 38, 47–8, 135, 149
terminals, 12–13, 45–6, 50, *50*, 55, 56
    on mainframe, 60
    on mini, 61, 62
    on networks, 62–3
text manipulation, 3, 4, 113–15, 138,
    186
touch screen, 49, 108
track, 67
tractor feeders, 72–3, *73*, 79
translator, 58
type styles, 71
typewriters
    electric, 2
    electronic, 4
    manual, 4
    compared with word processors, 3–4,
        20, 49, 54, 83

underlining, 44–5, 114, 122, 131, 191
updating, 17, 29–31, *30*, 174
upper case, 36, 99, 114
user friendly software, 59

variables, 20
VDU (visual display unit), 50, 88
vertical
    lines, 149
    scrolling, 36
voice input, 14

wide screen, 36, 149
widows and orphans, 103, 190
Winchester disks, 68

word processor, *3*
   definition, 4–5
   development, 2–3
   compared with typewriter, 3–4, 20,
     49, 54, 83

workflow, 169–70
workstations, 61, 62, 83–5, *84*
wraparound, 35, 108
write commands, 115, 131
write-protect label, 66